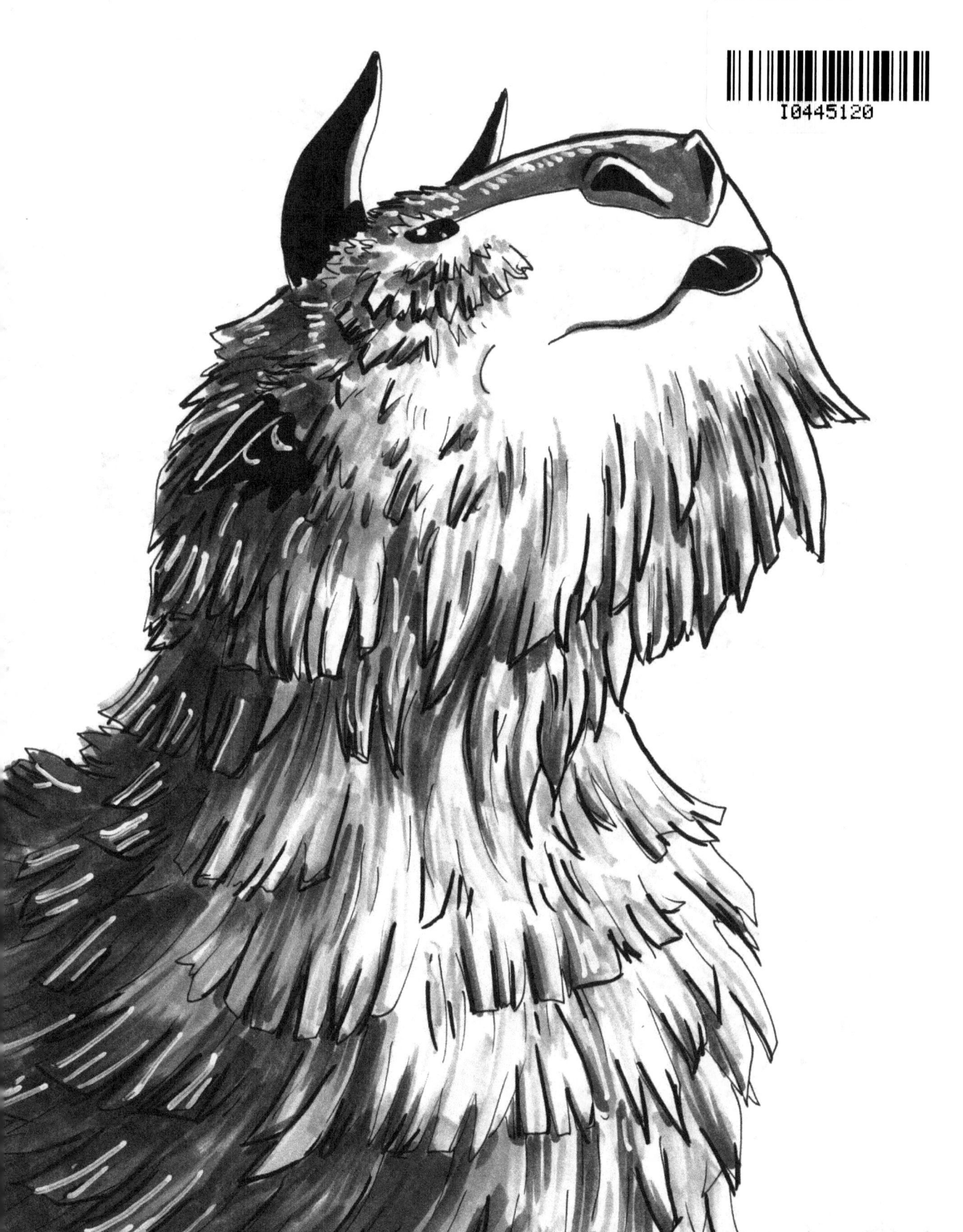

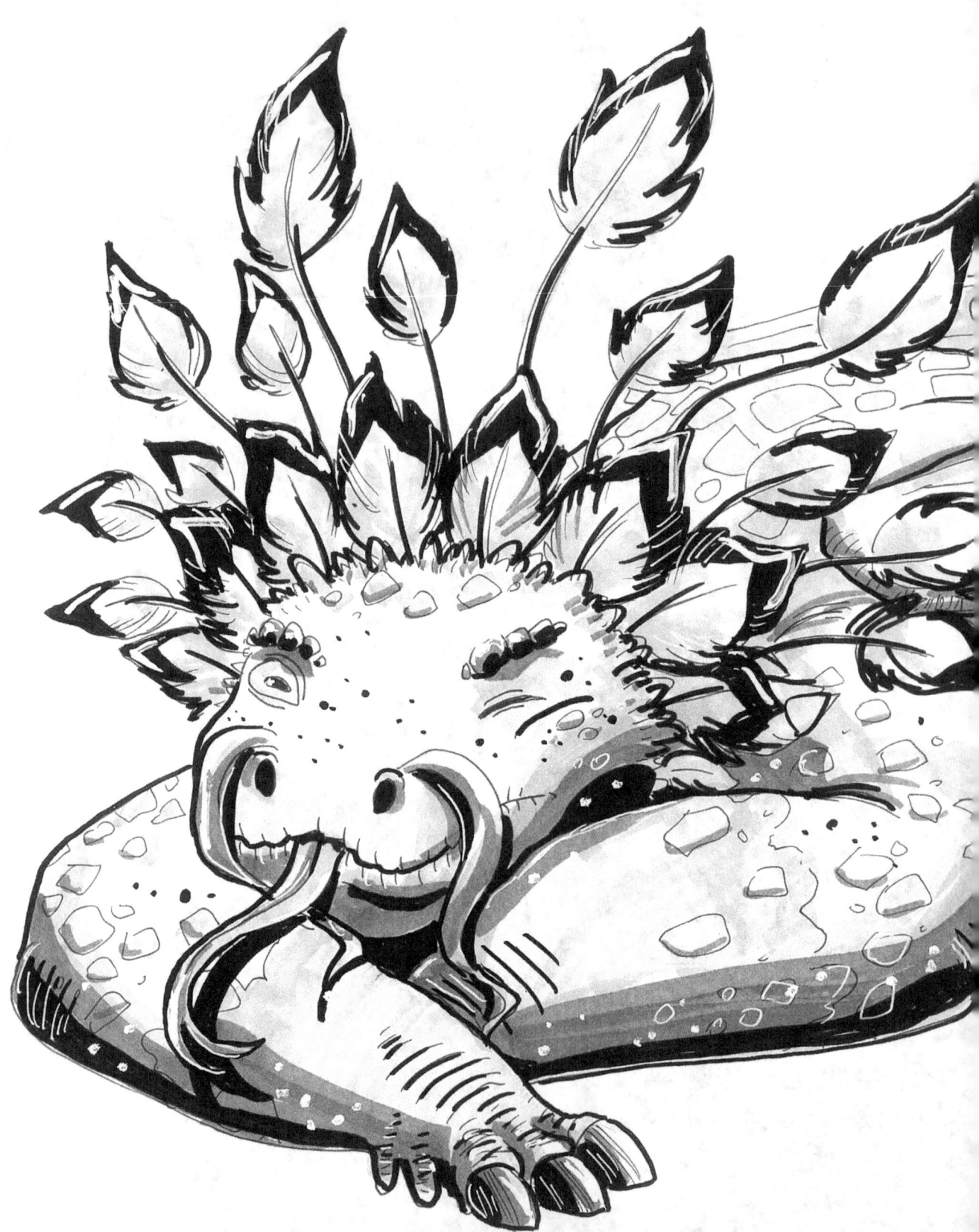

Thank you so much for purchasing my artbook:

Fantasy in Monokrom

Ink Art by Diane Ramic: Vol. 1

Your support means a lot to me!

In this collection, you can find the bulk of my fantasy-themed black and white ink work I have drawn over the last few years, spanning from daily marker drawings of dragons done for a month-long challenge, to stock art created for individuals to use in their own games and stories.

If you'd like to see more of my work, you can either contact me via email at dianeramic@gmail.com, or visit one of my online portfolios below!

dramic.wixsite.com/home

dianeramic.tumblr.com

diantimony.com

All illustrations copyright © Diane Ramic 2025. All rights reserved.

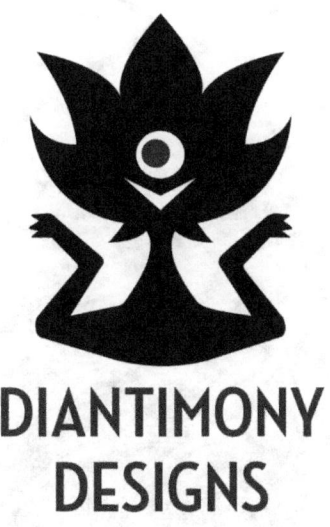

DIANTIMONY
DESIGNS

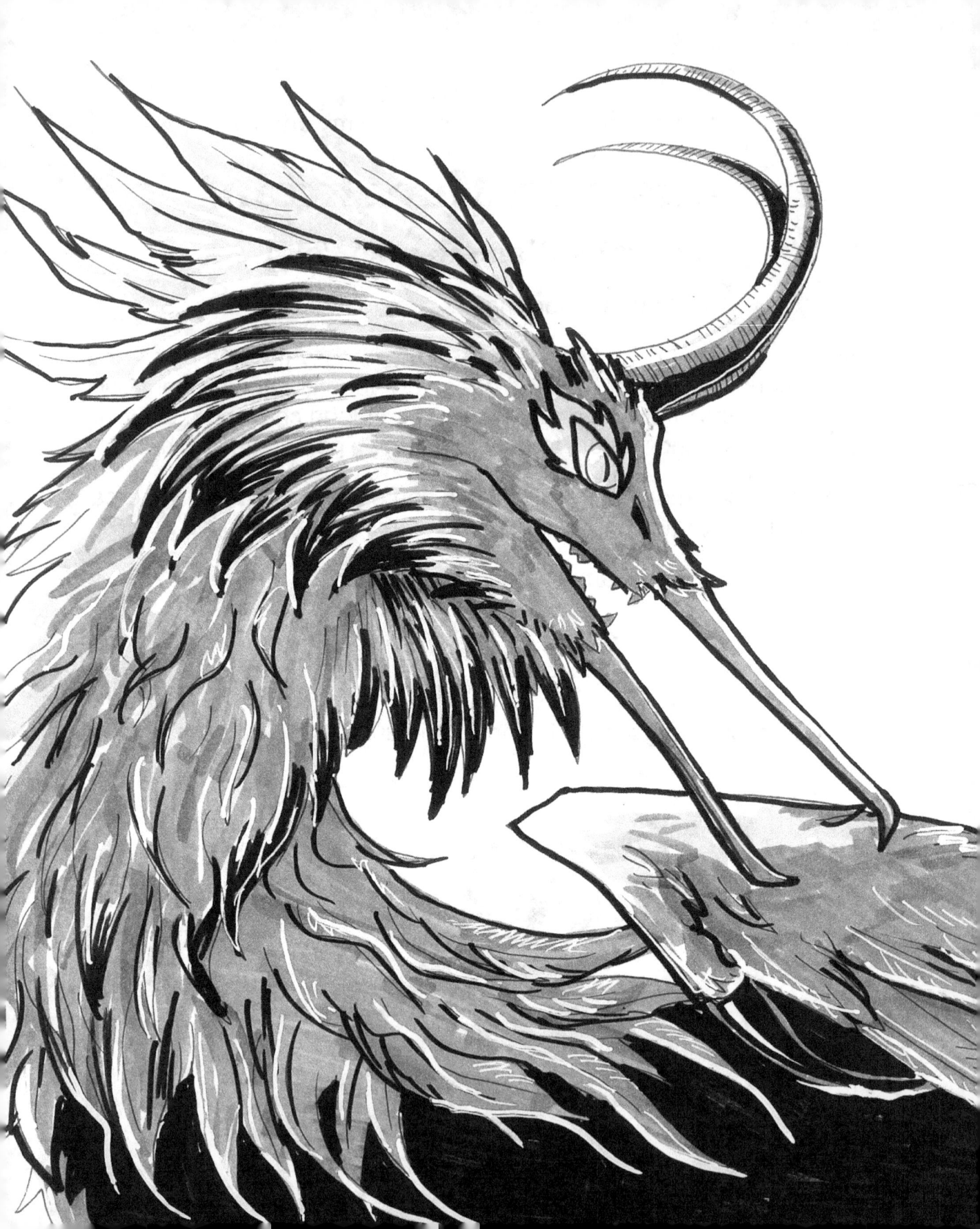

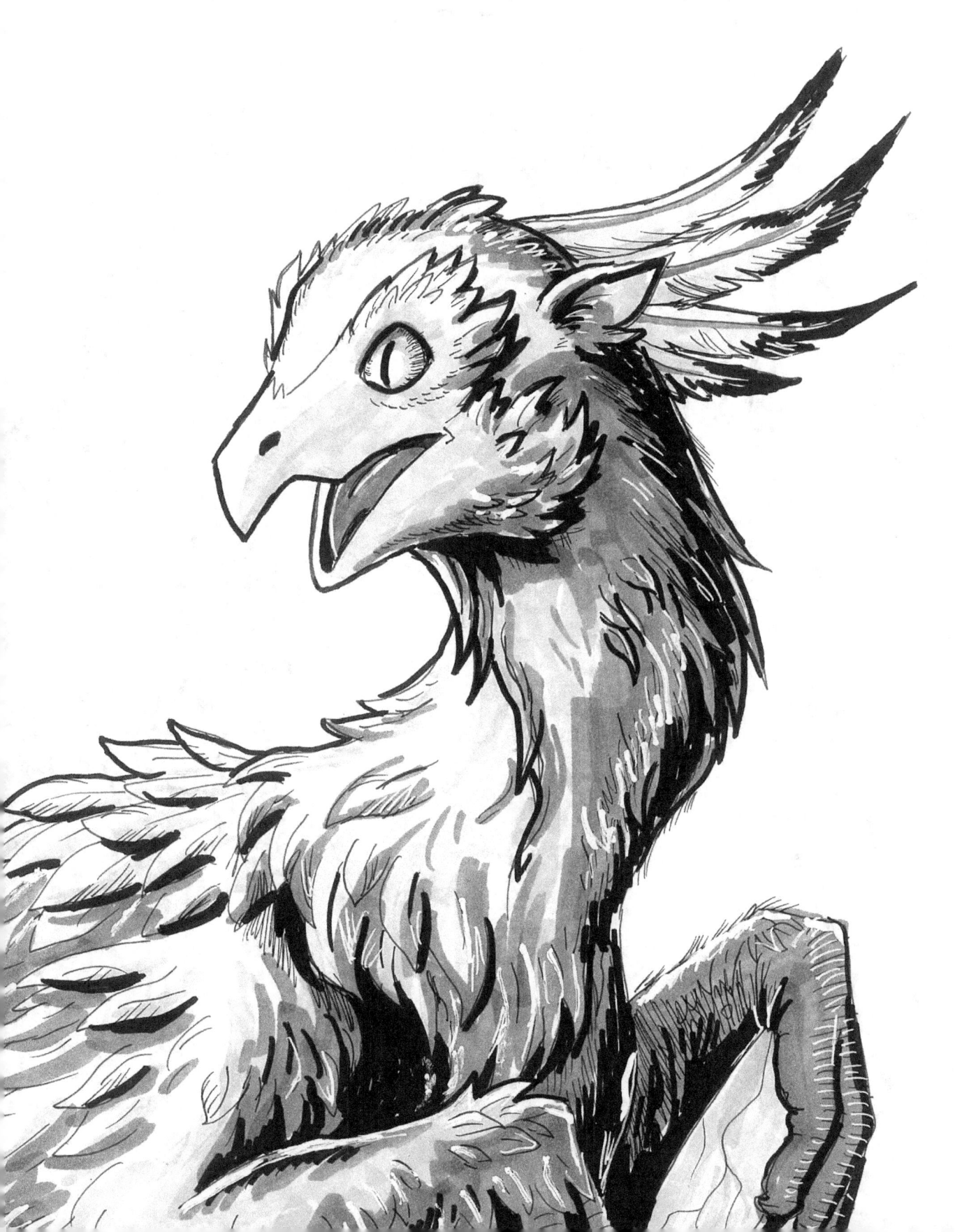

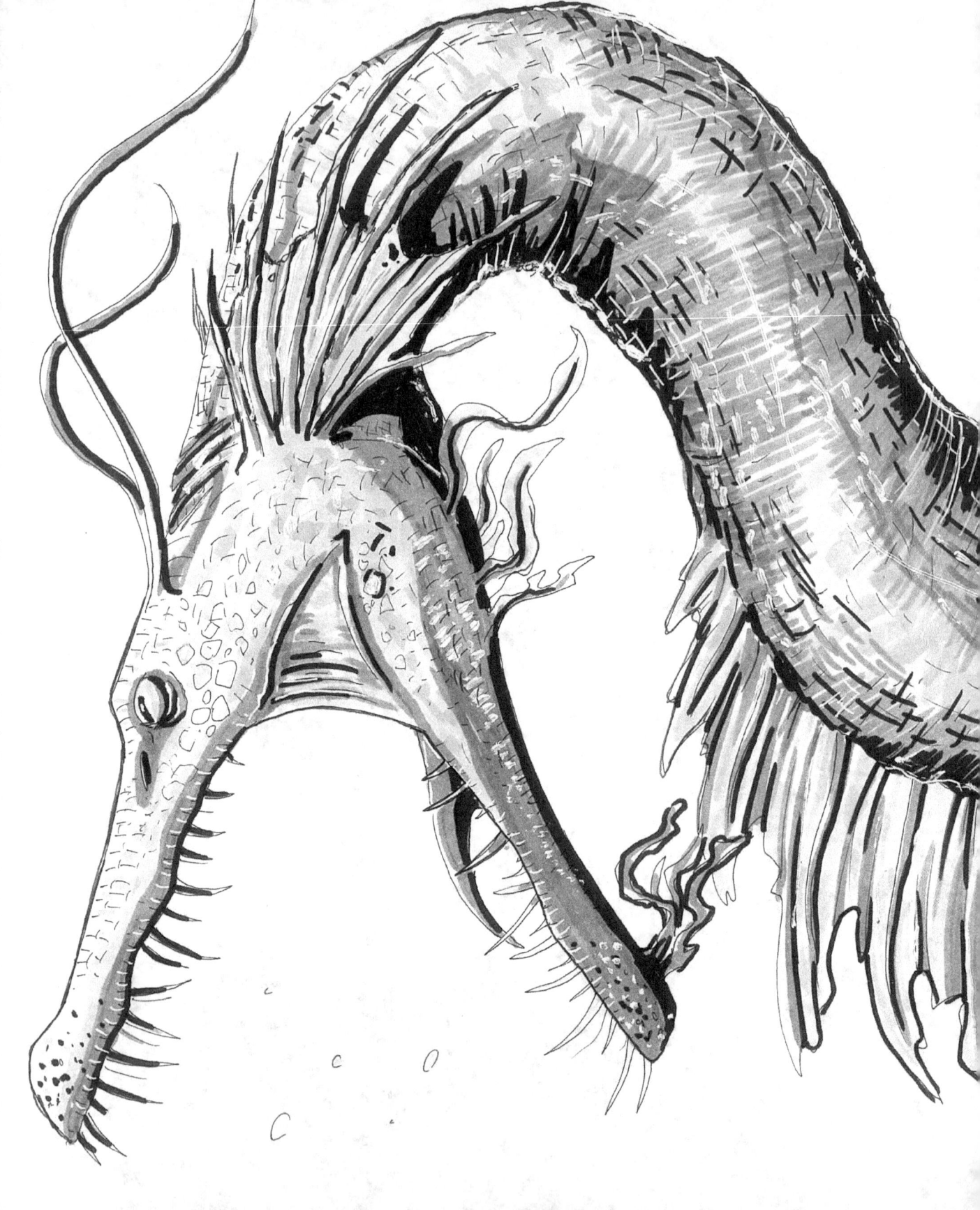

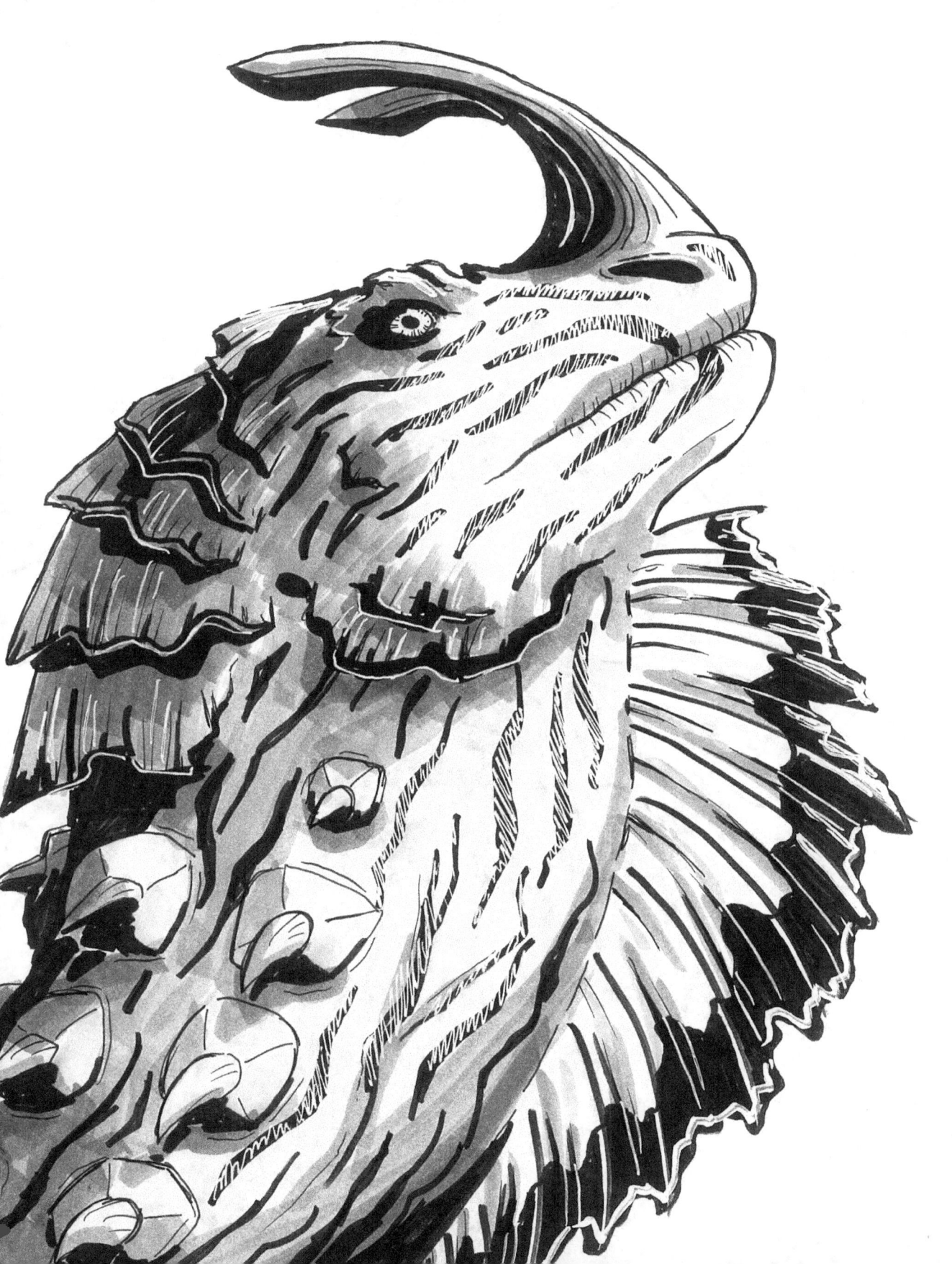

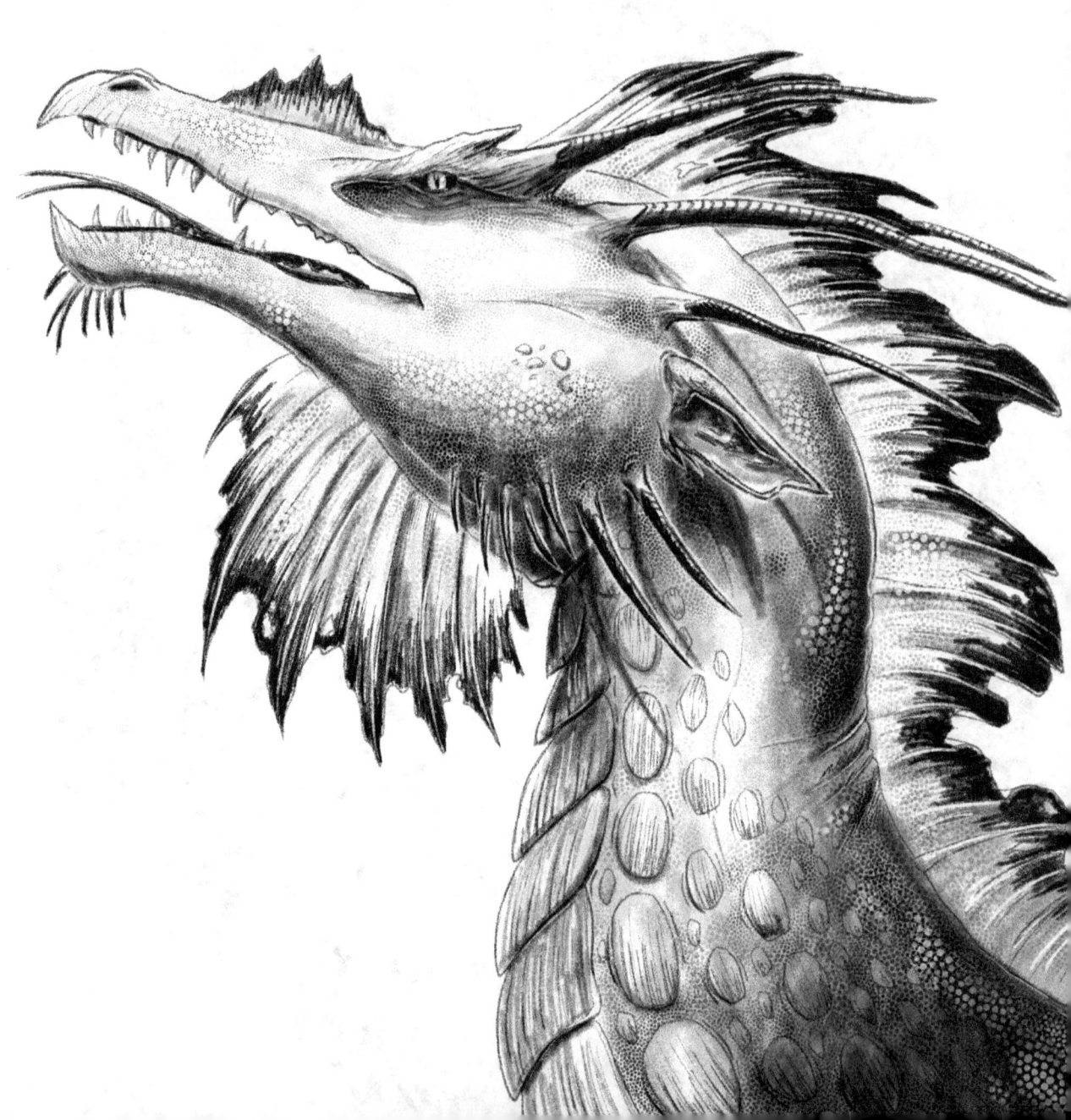

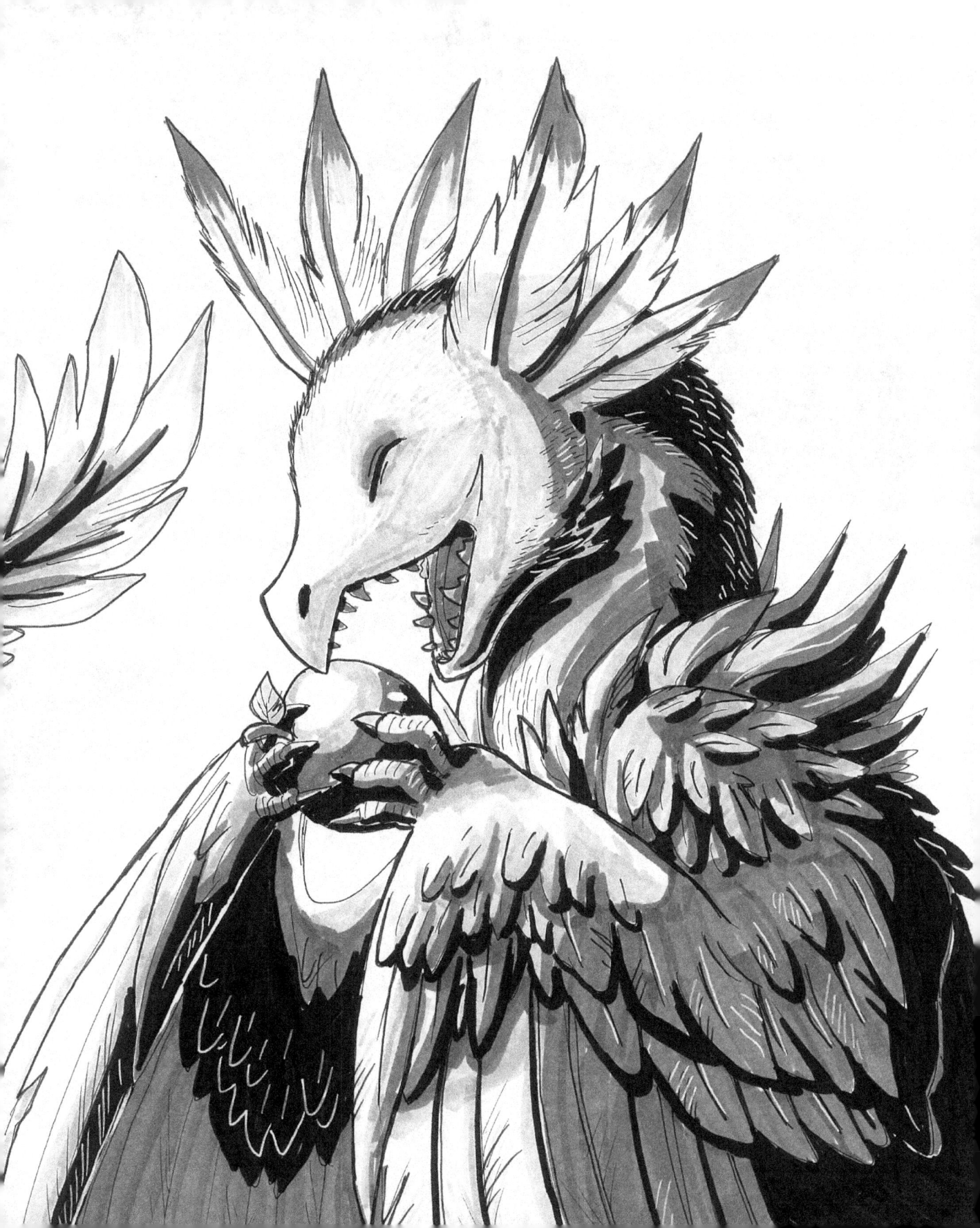

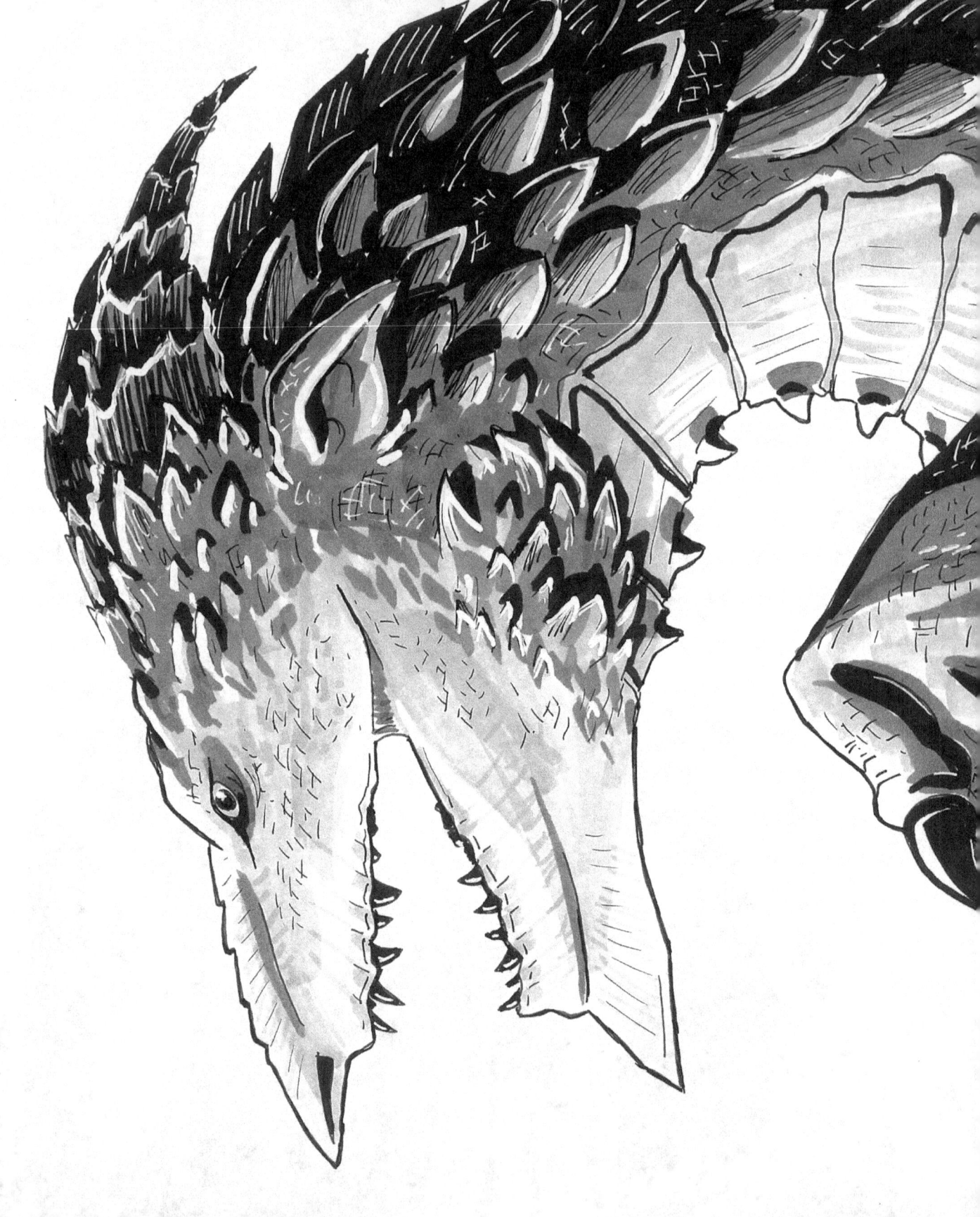

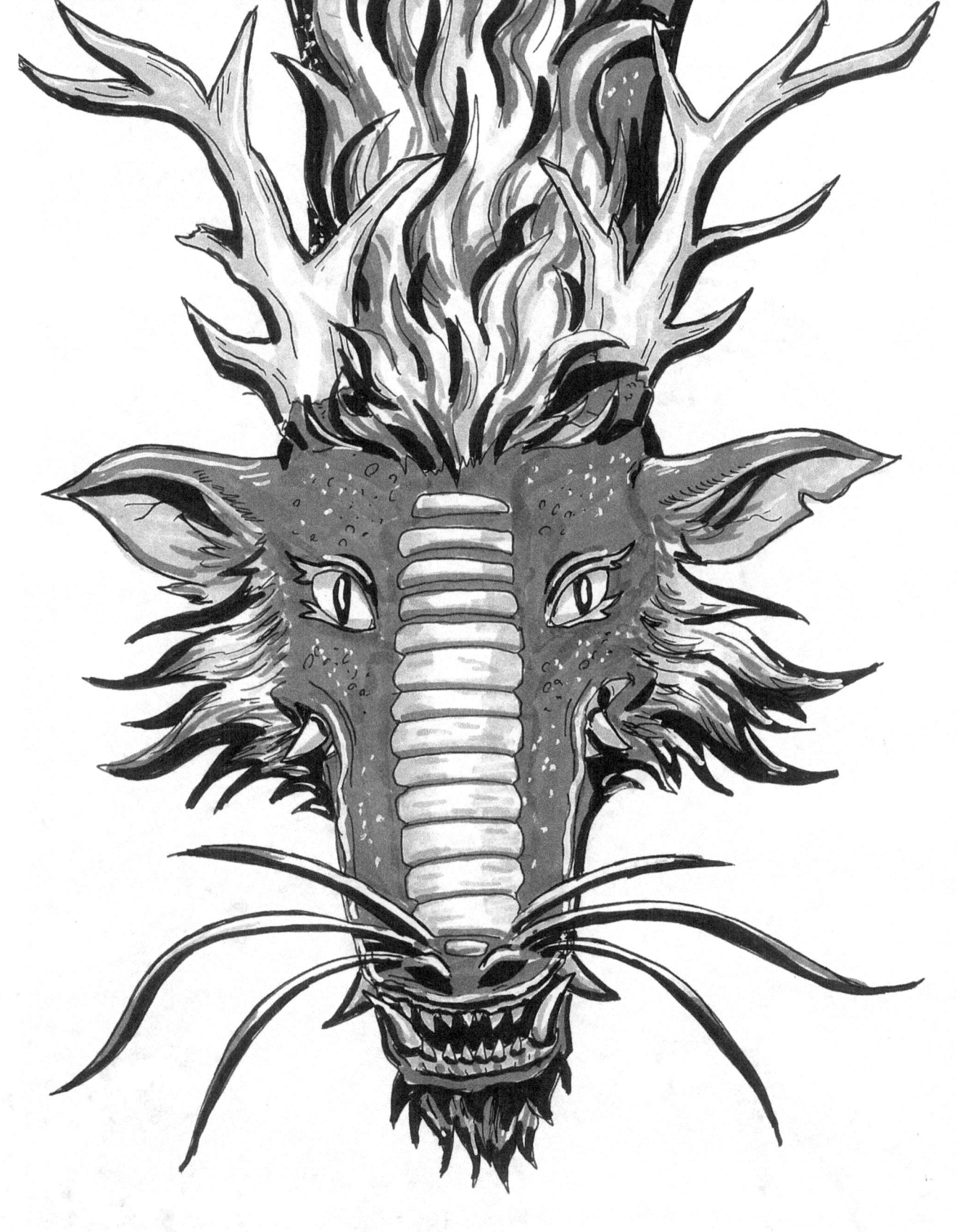

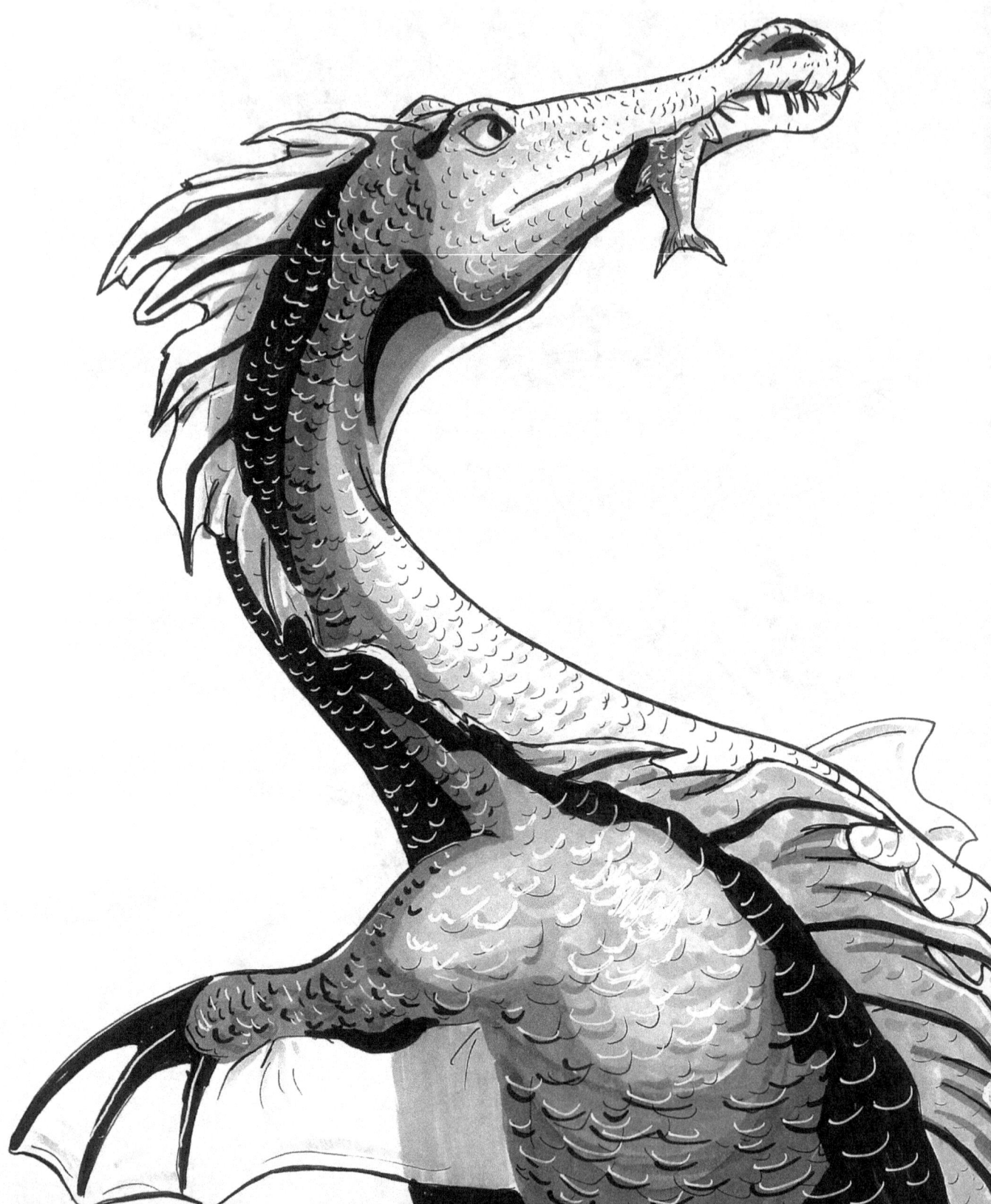

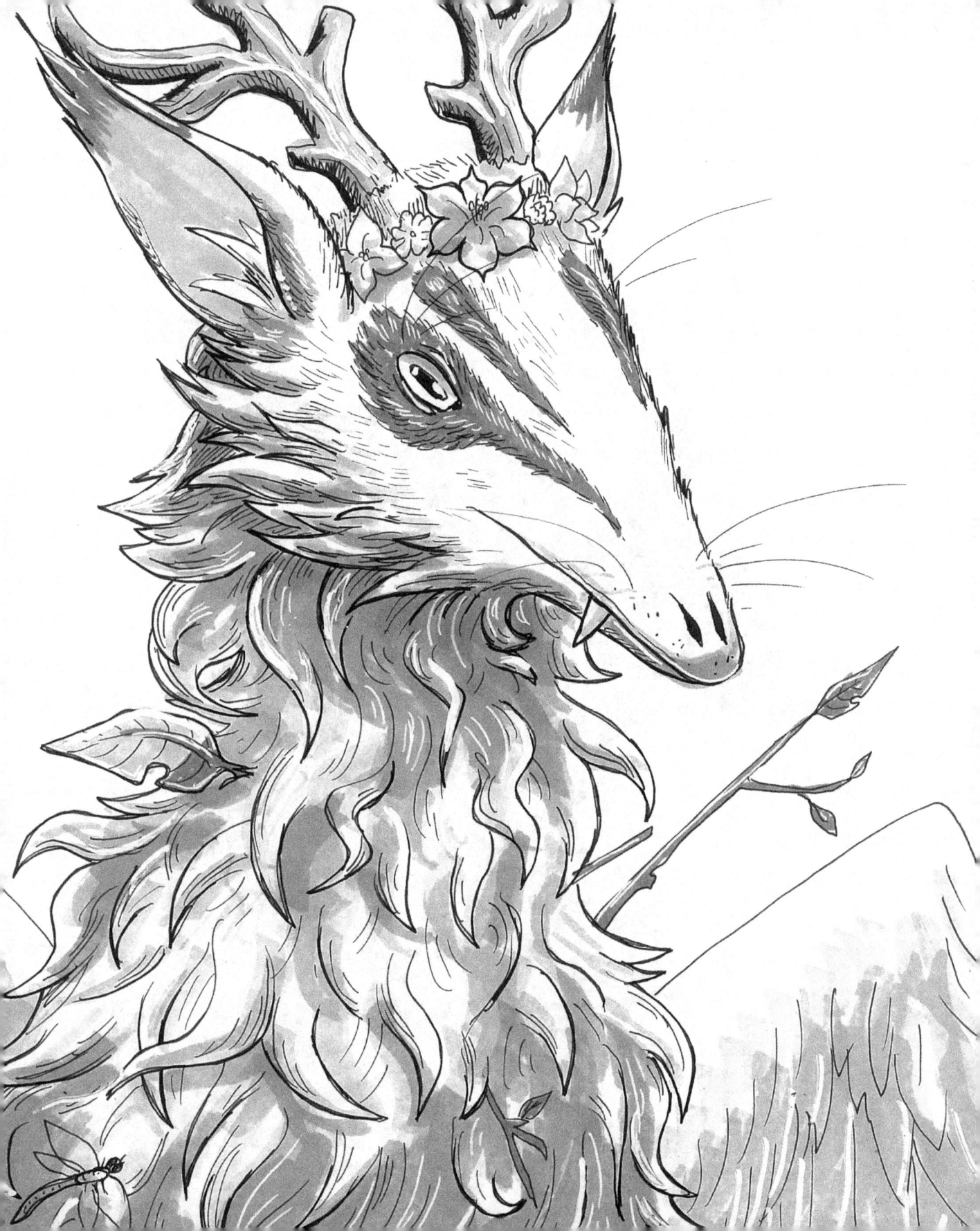

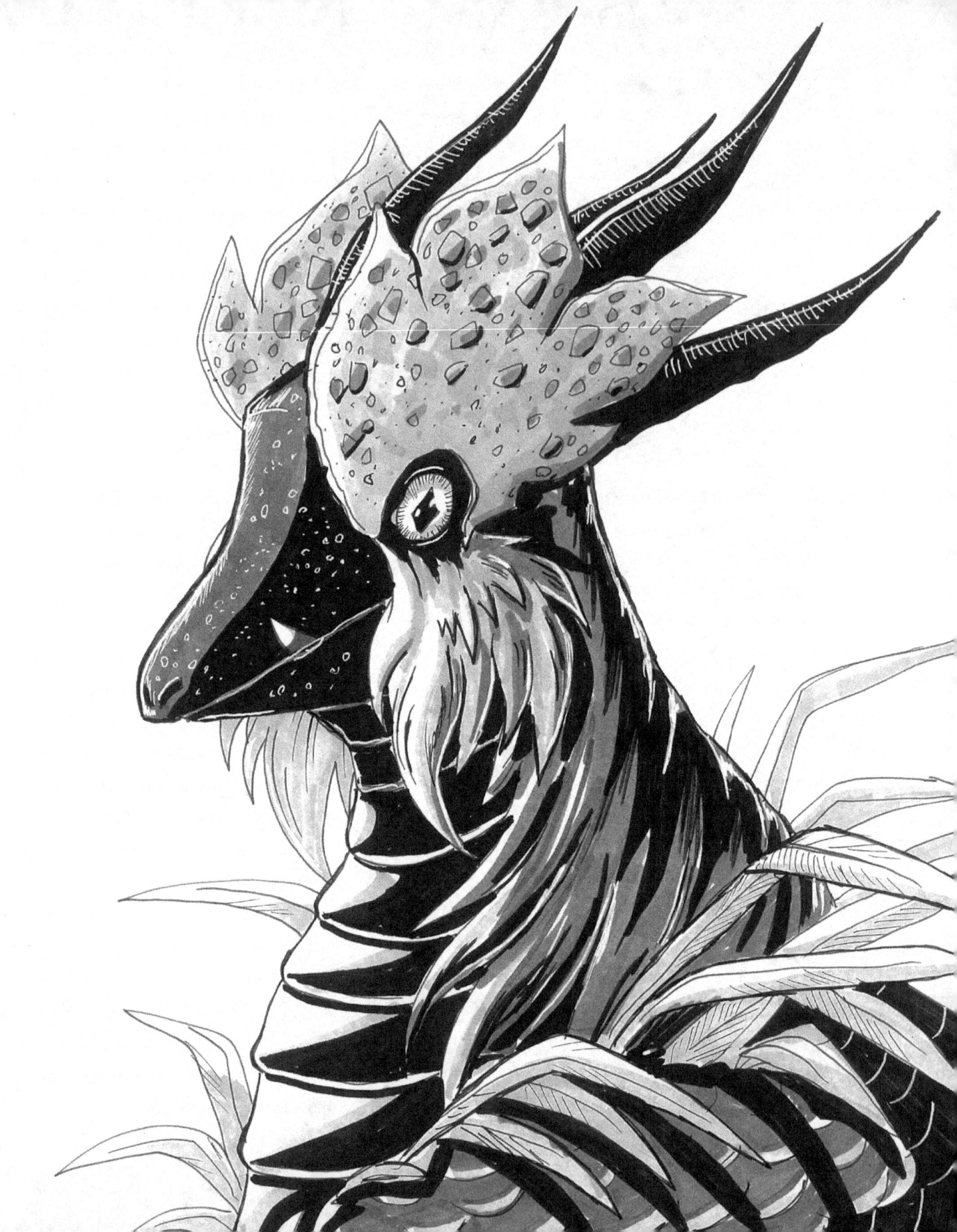

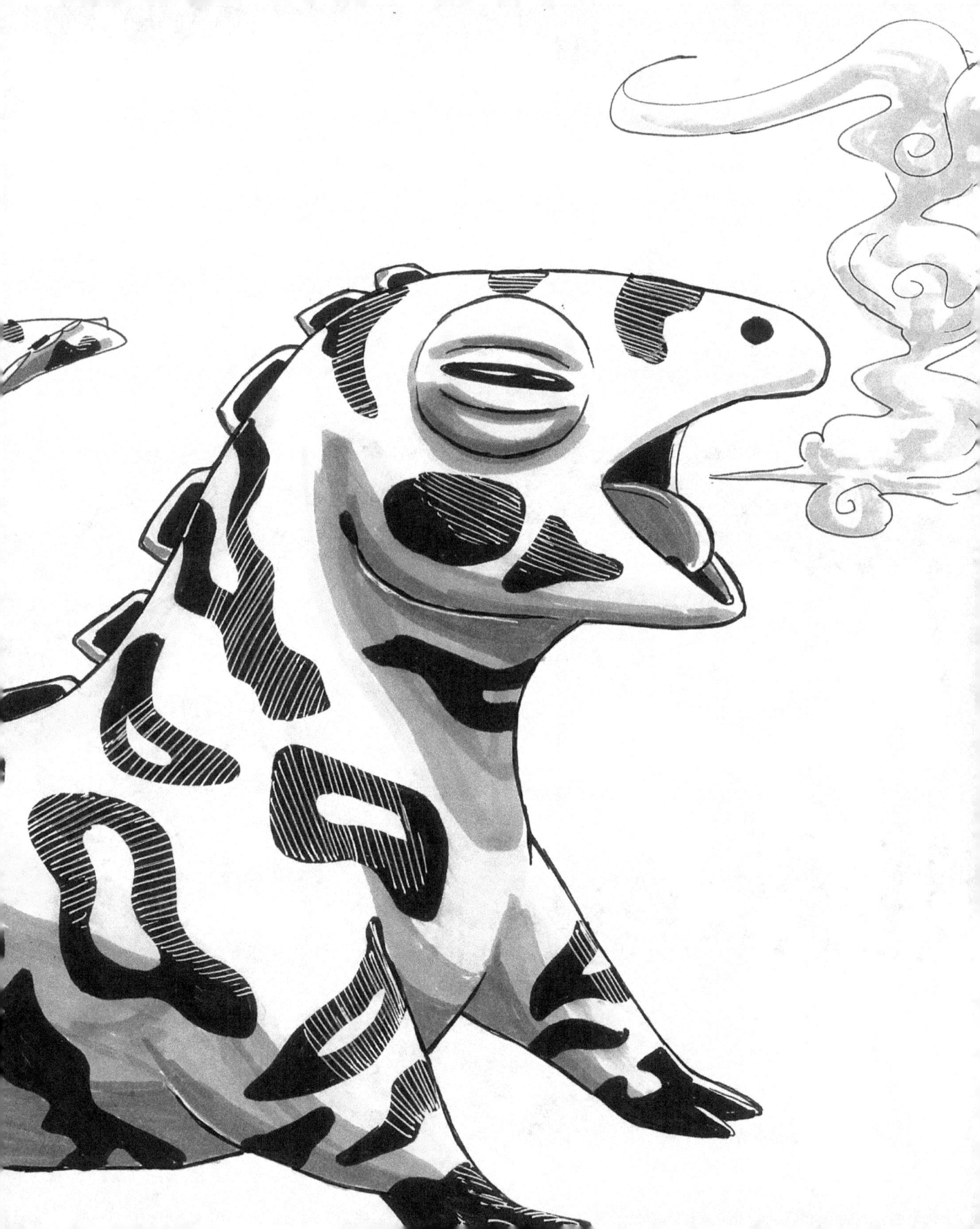

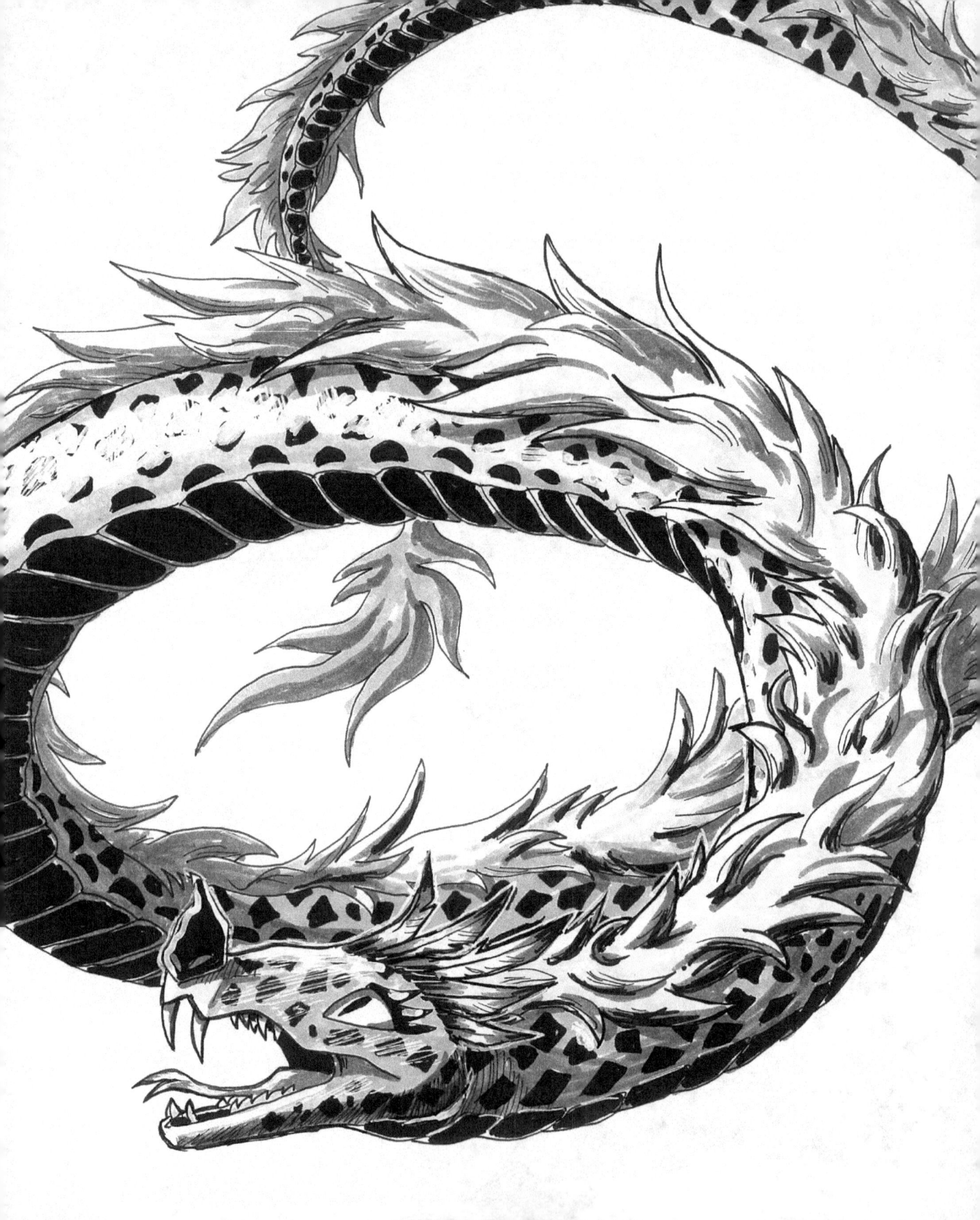

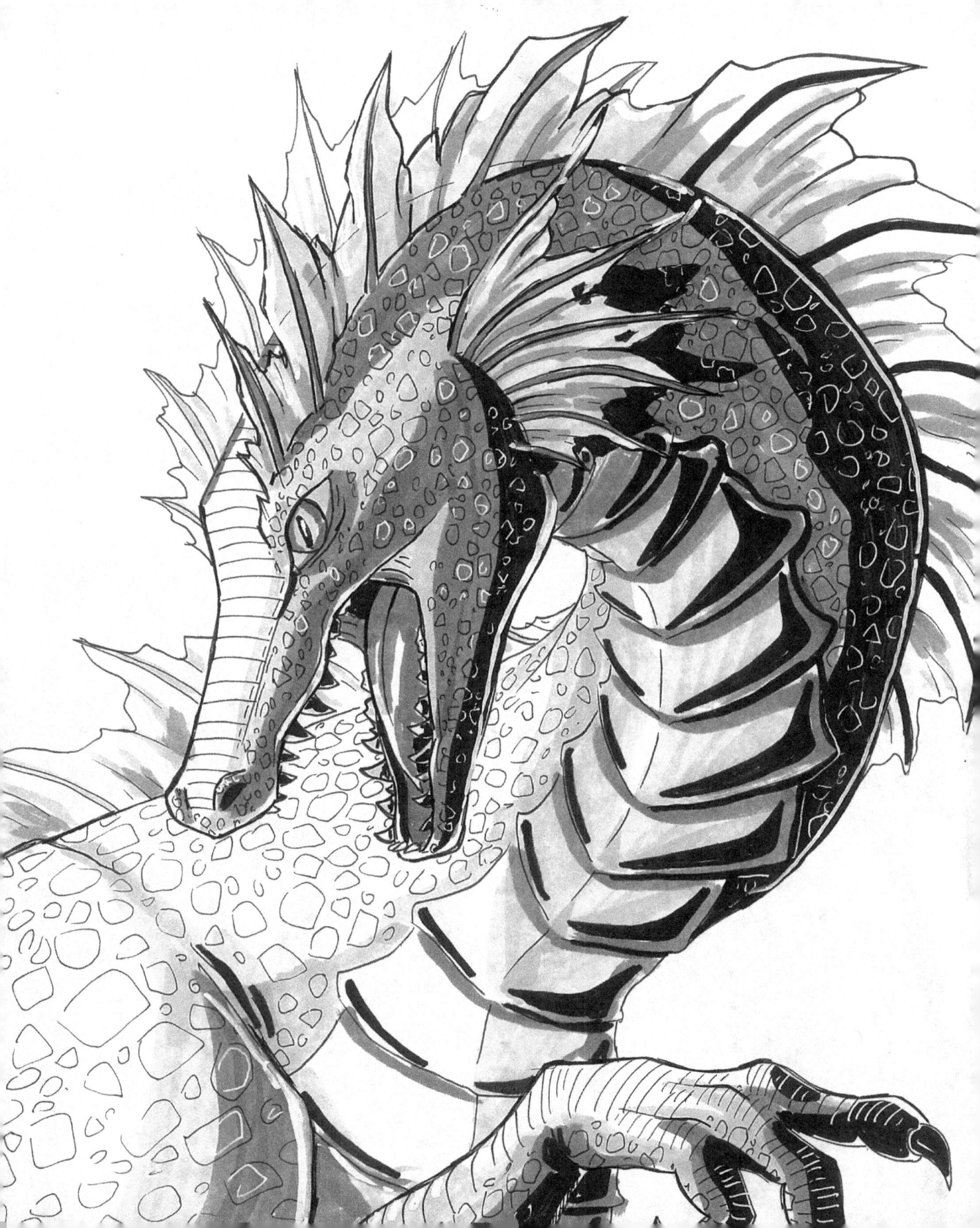

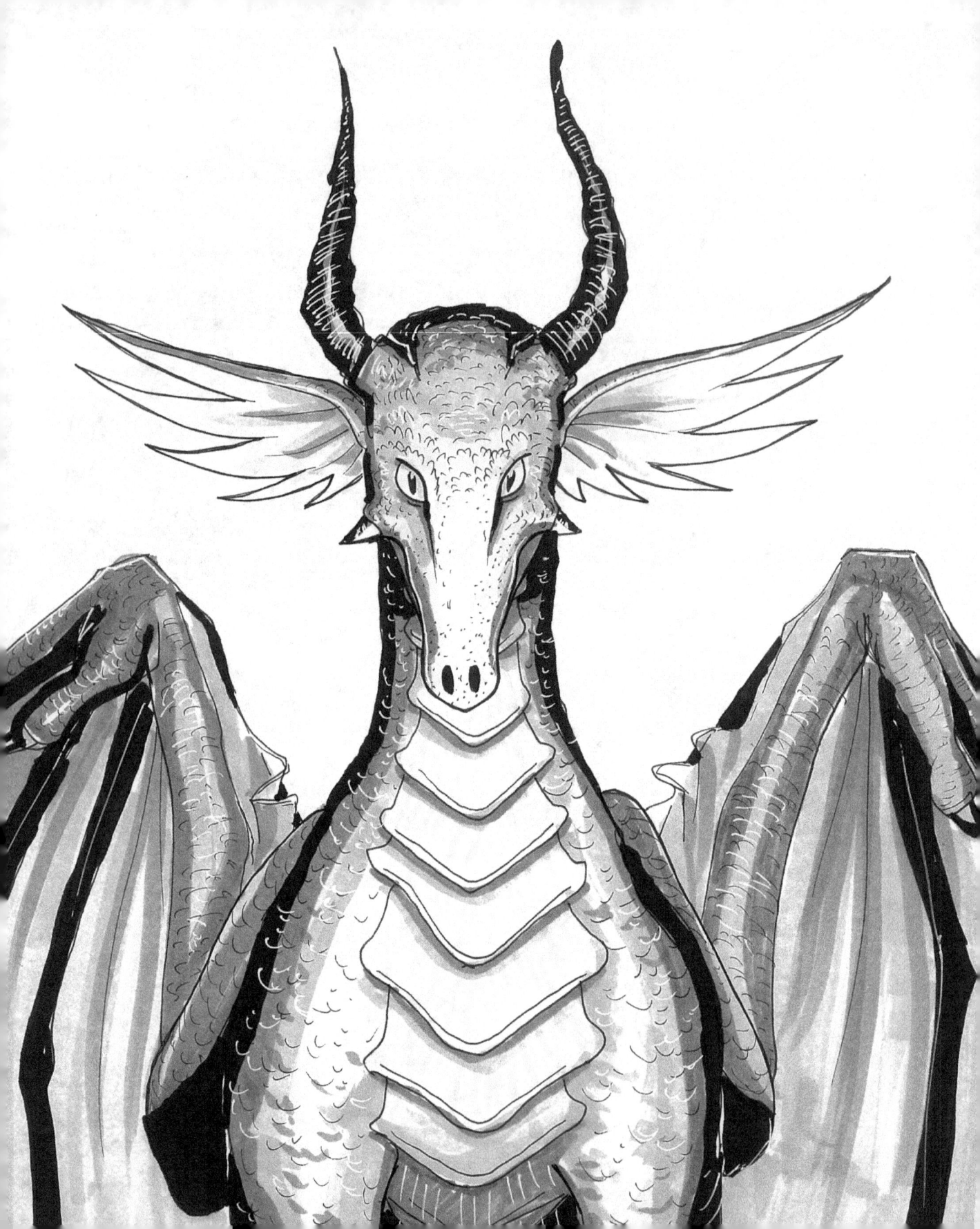

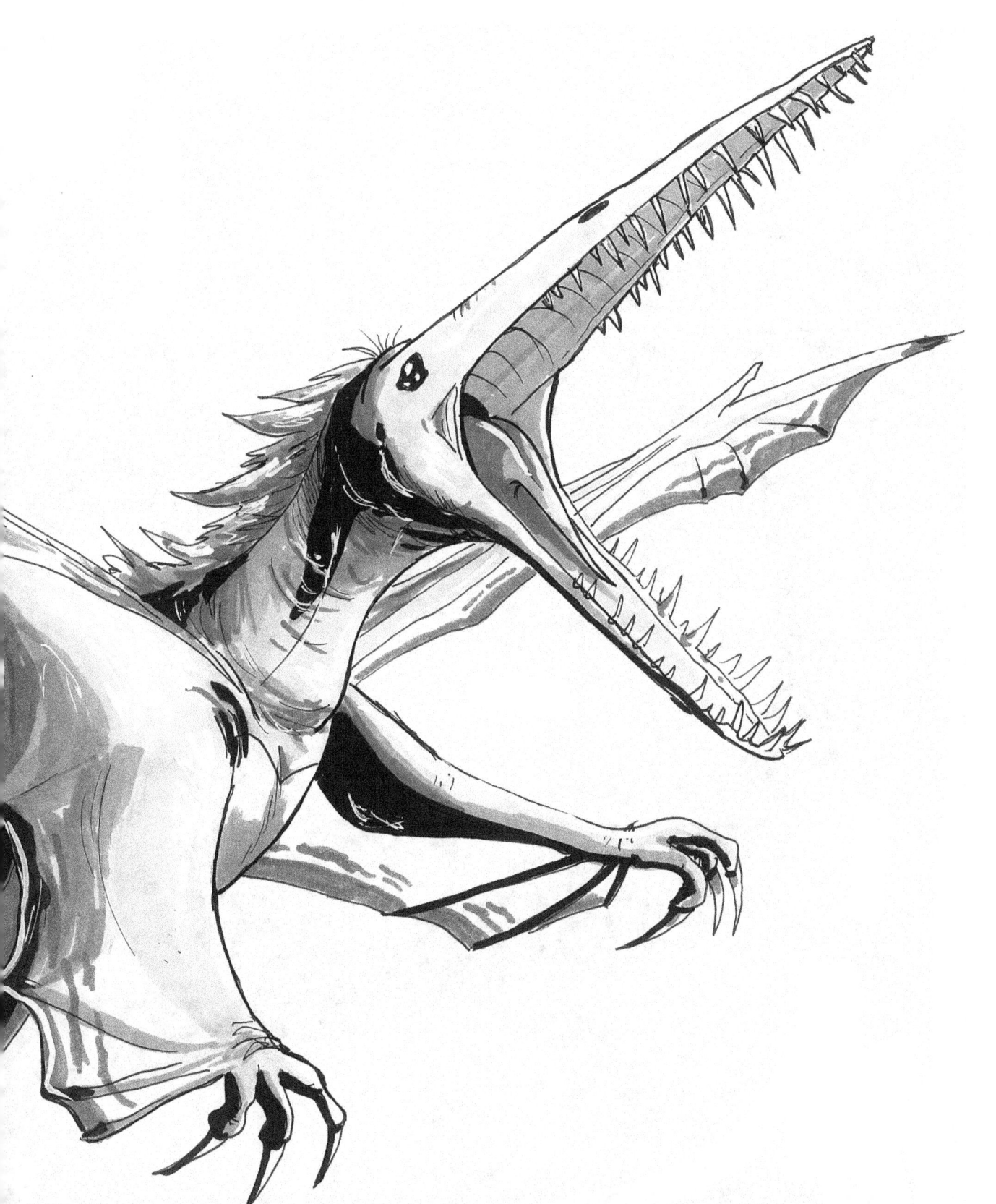

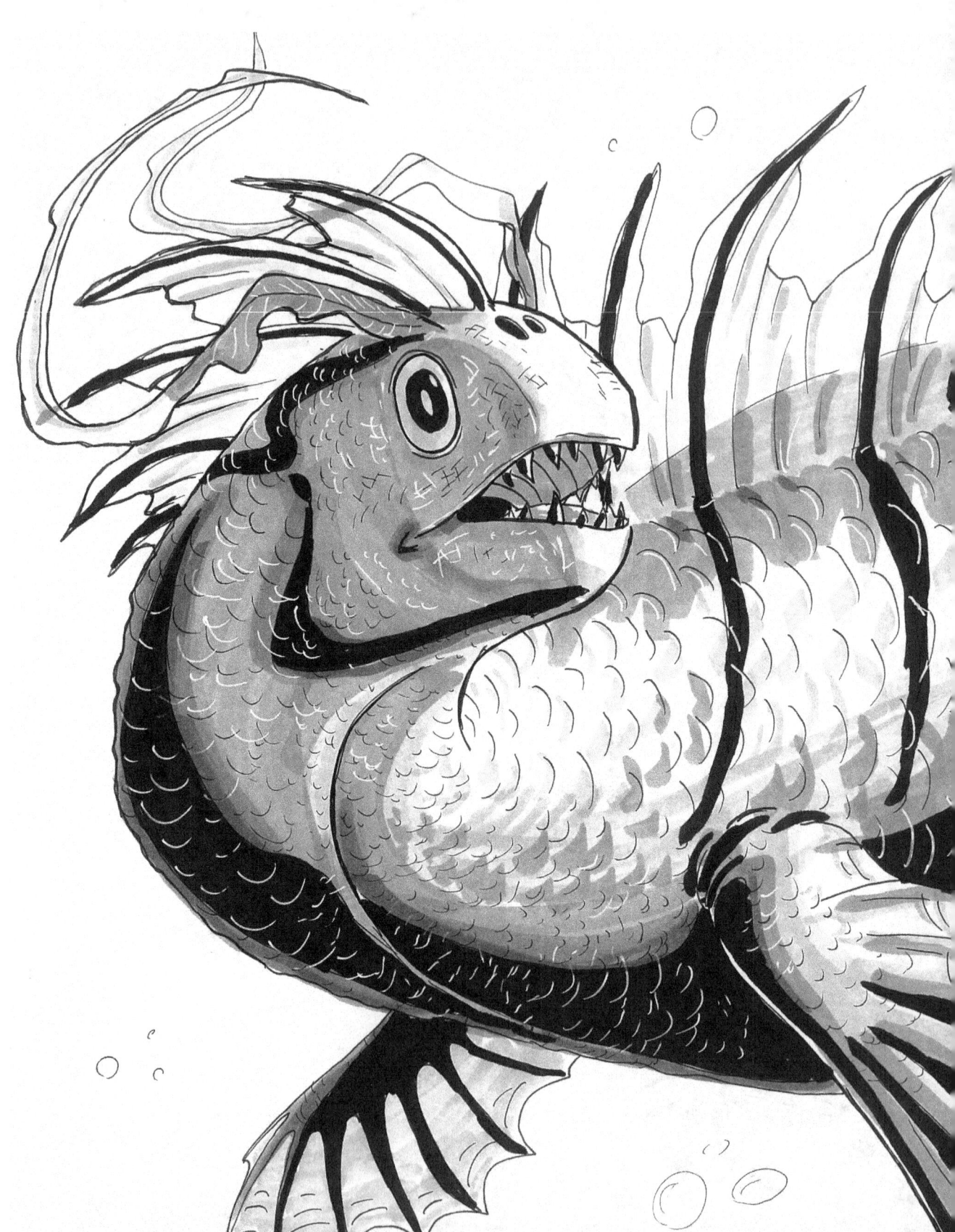

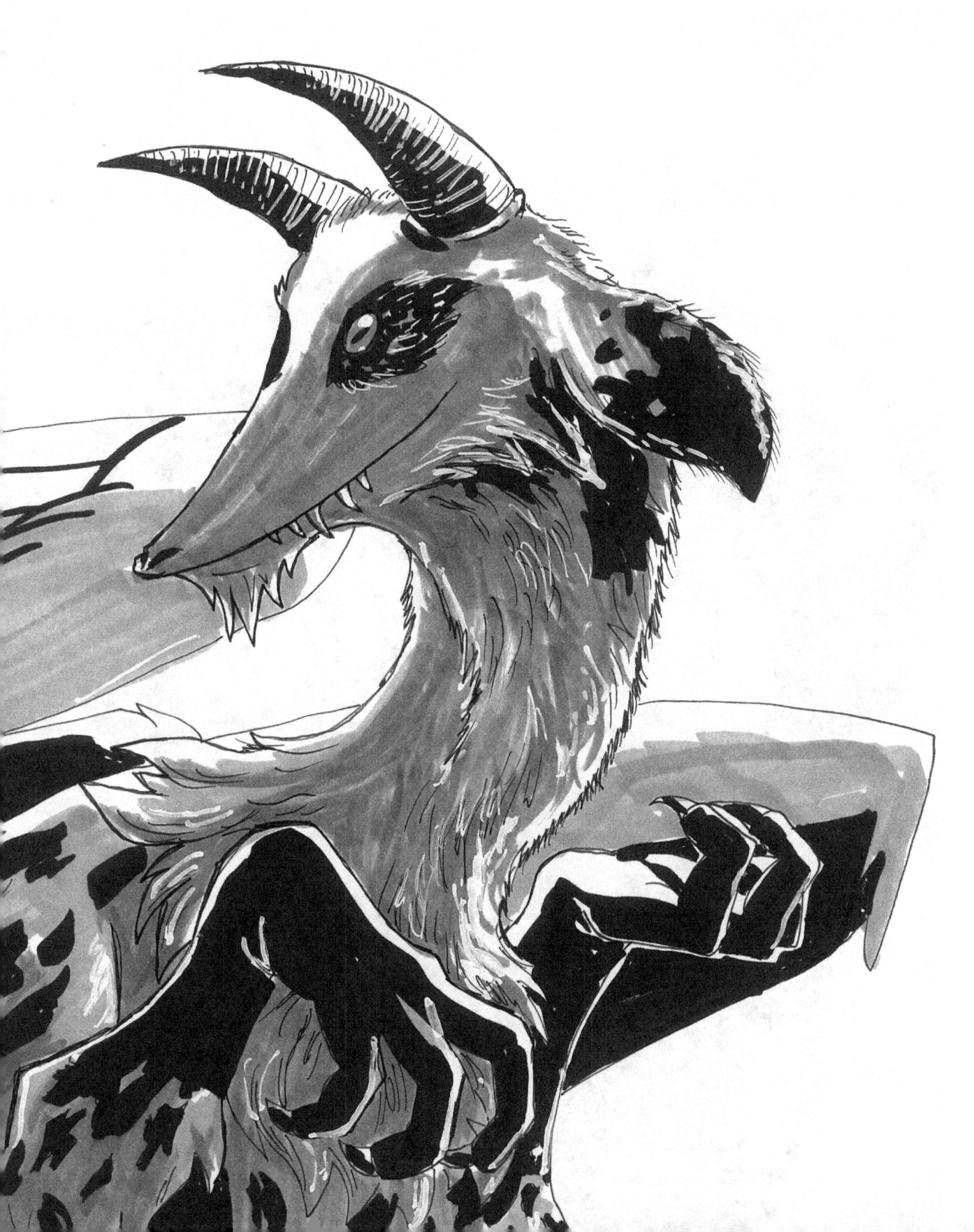

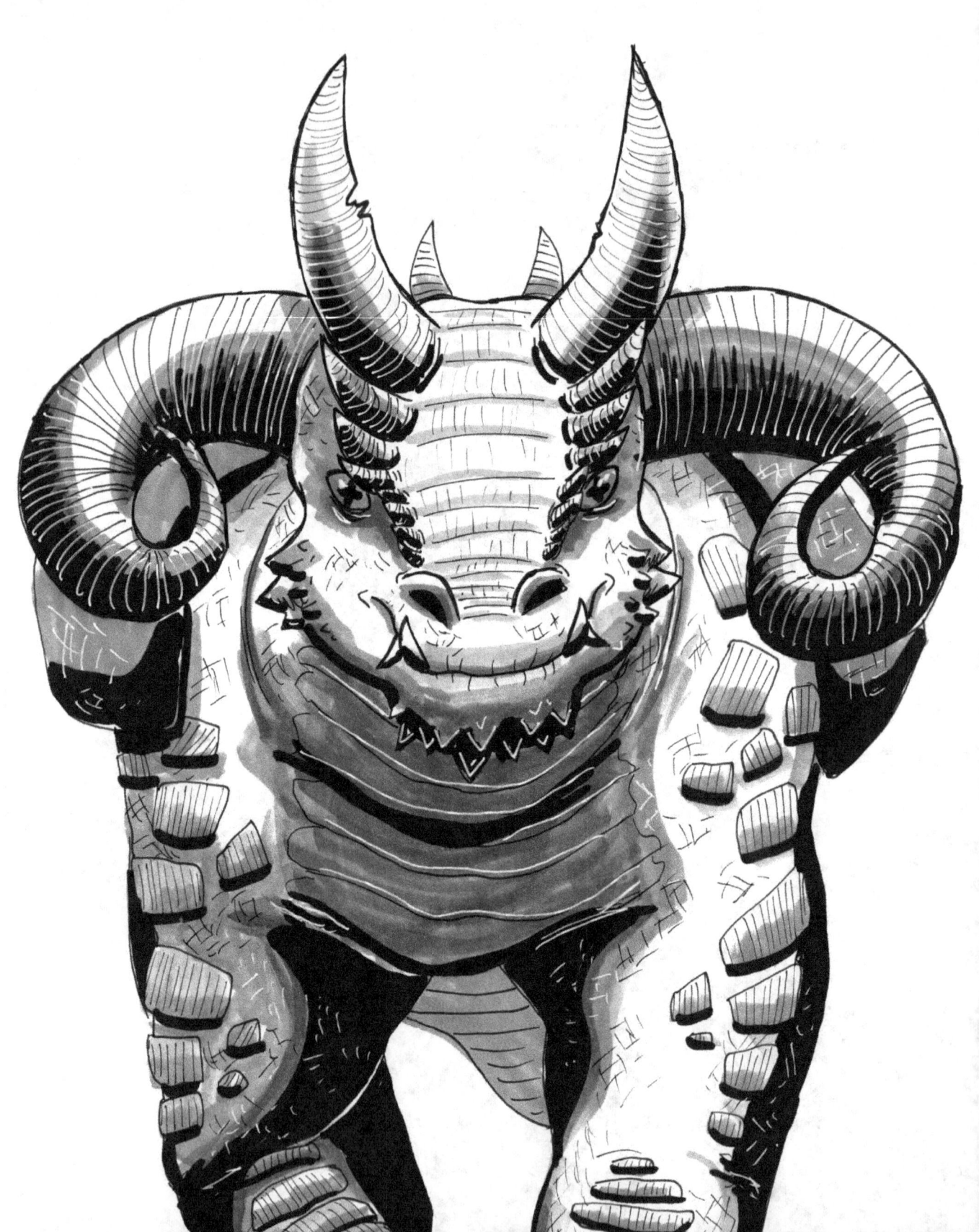

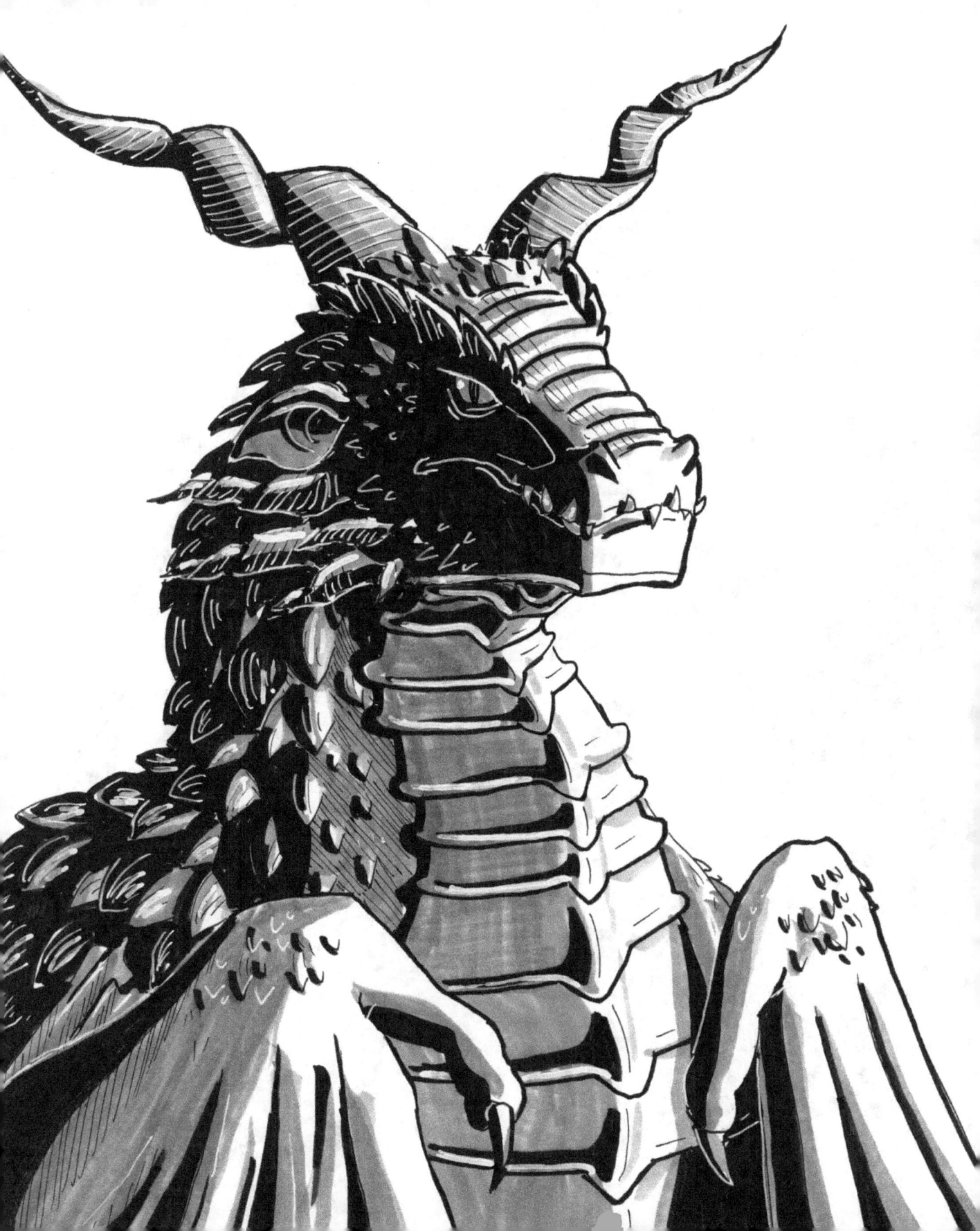

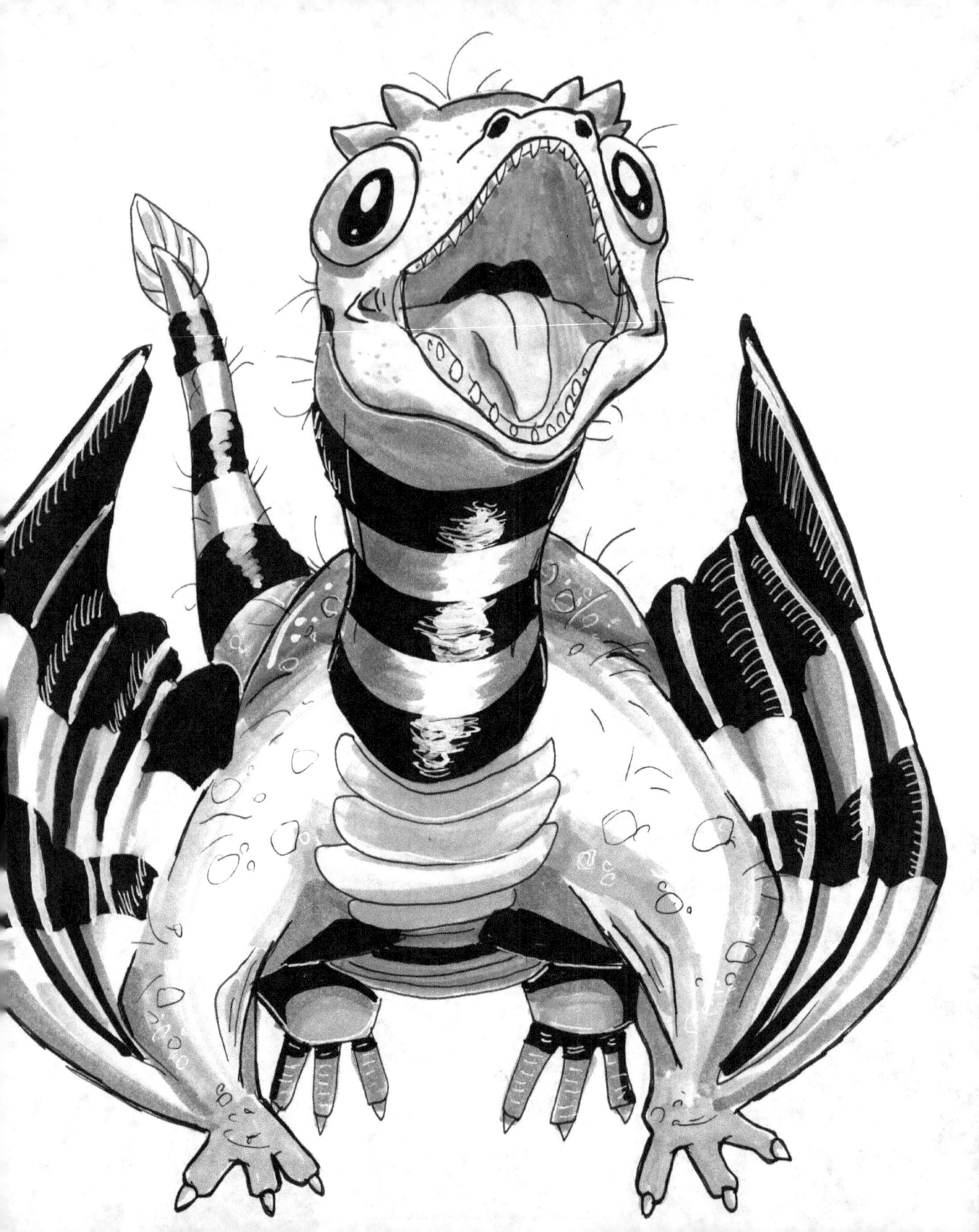

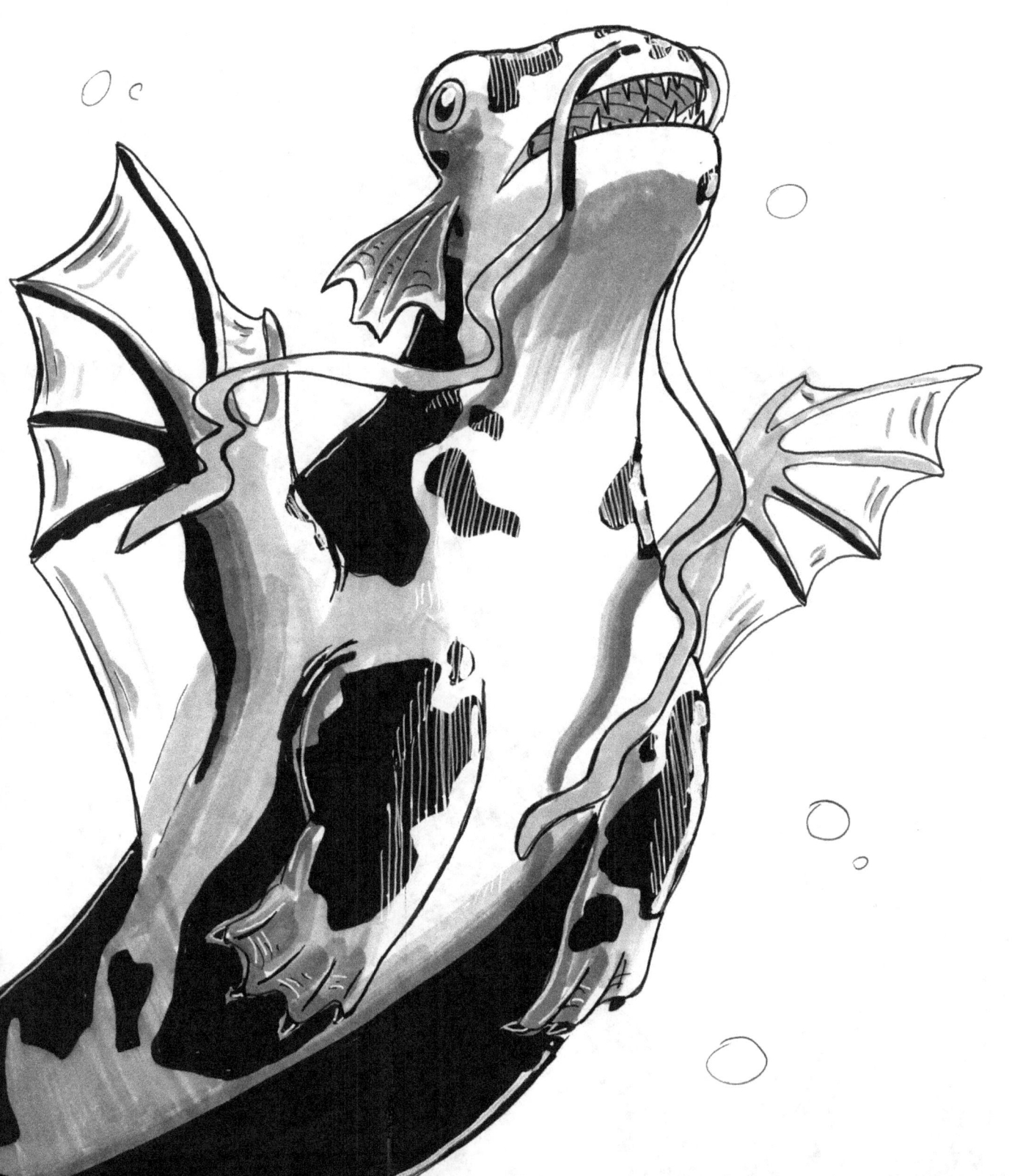

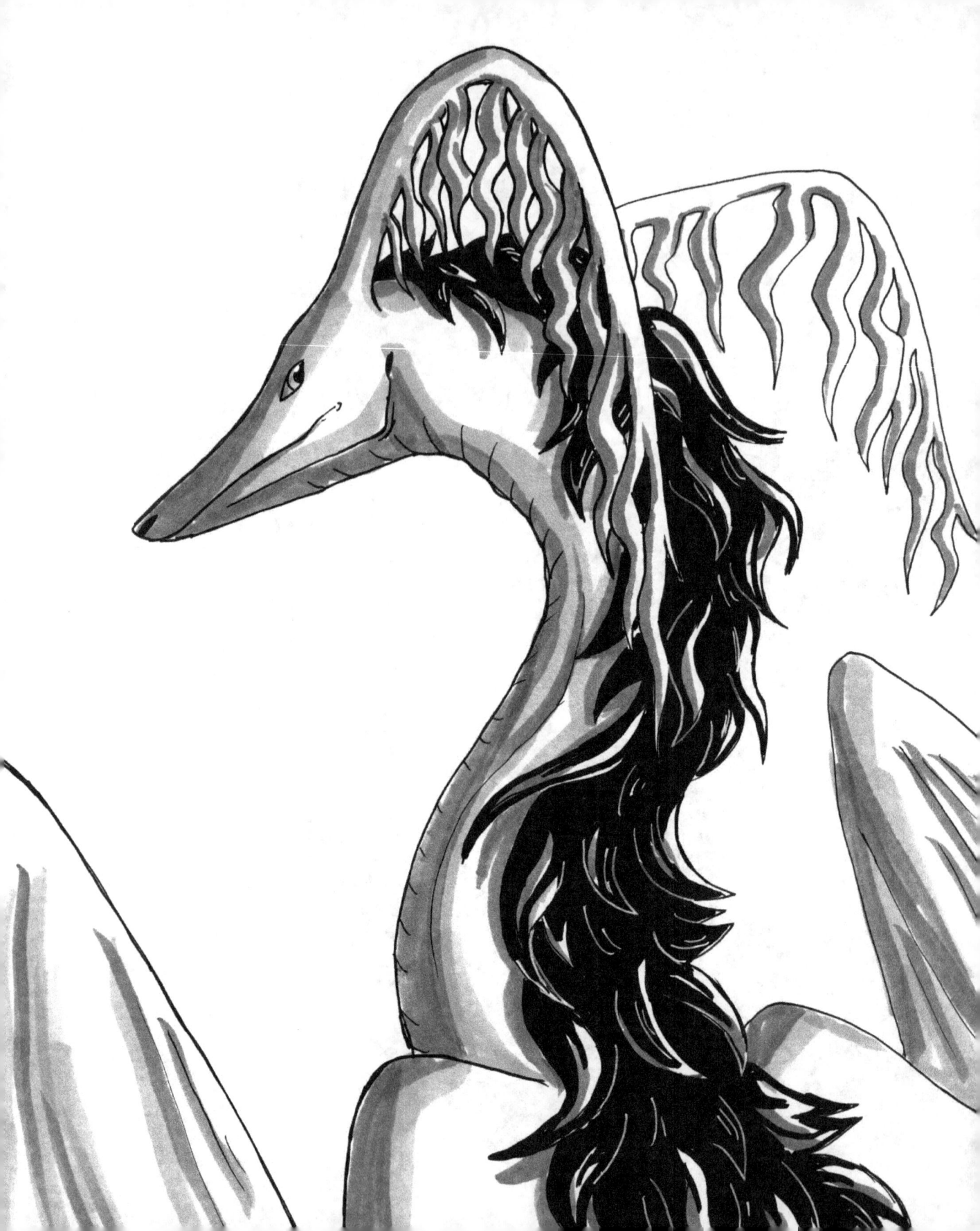

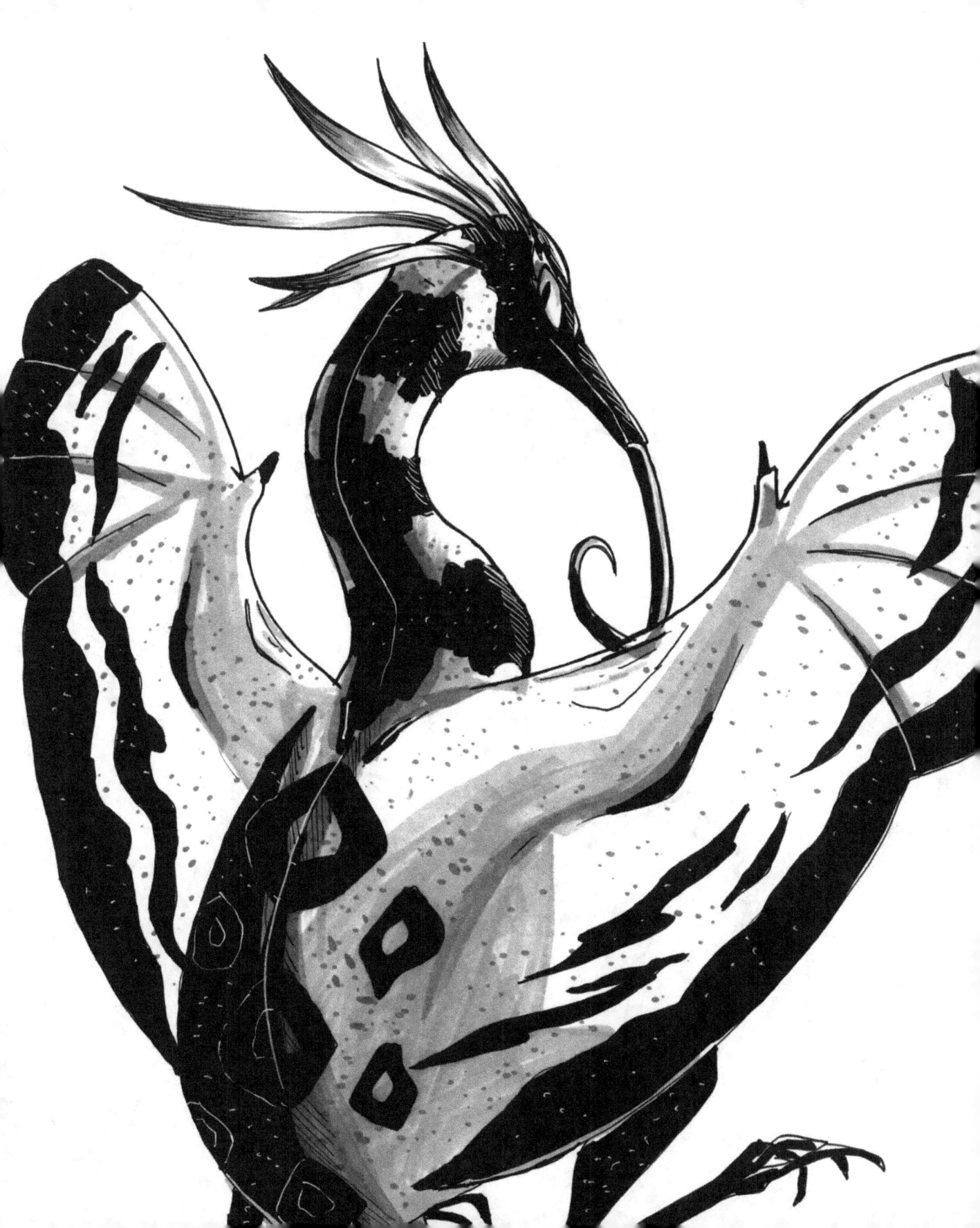

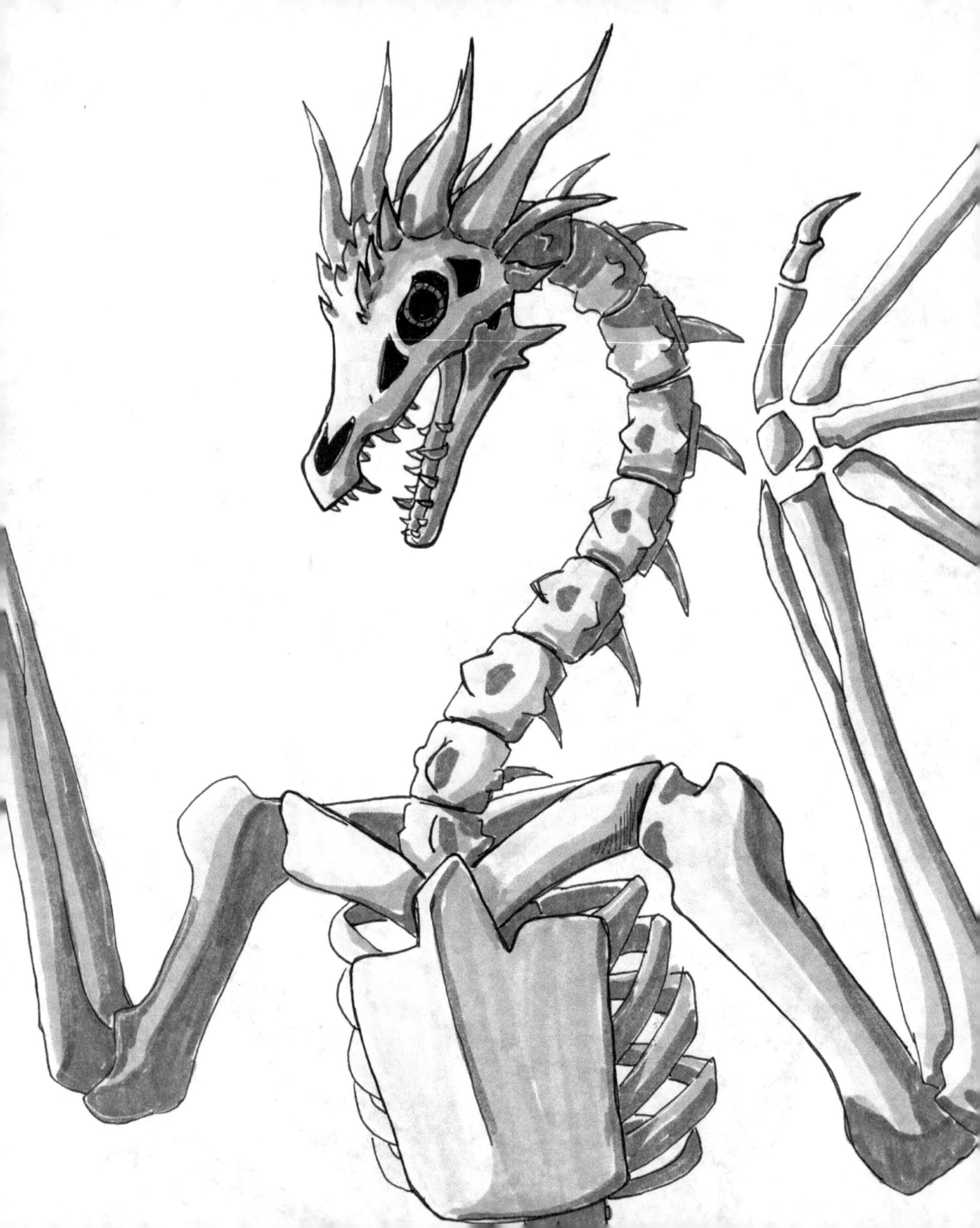

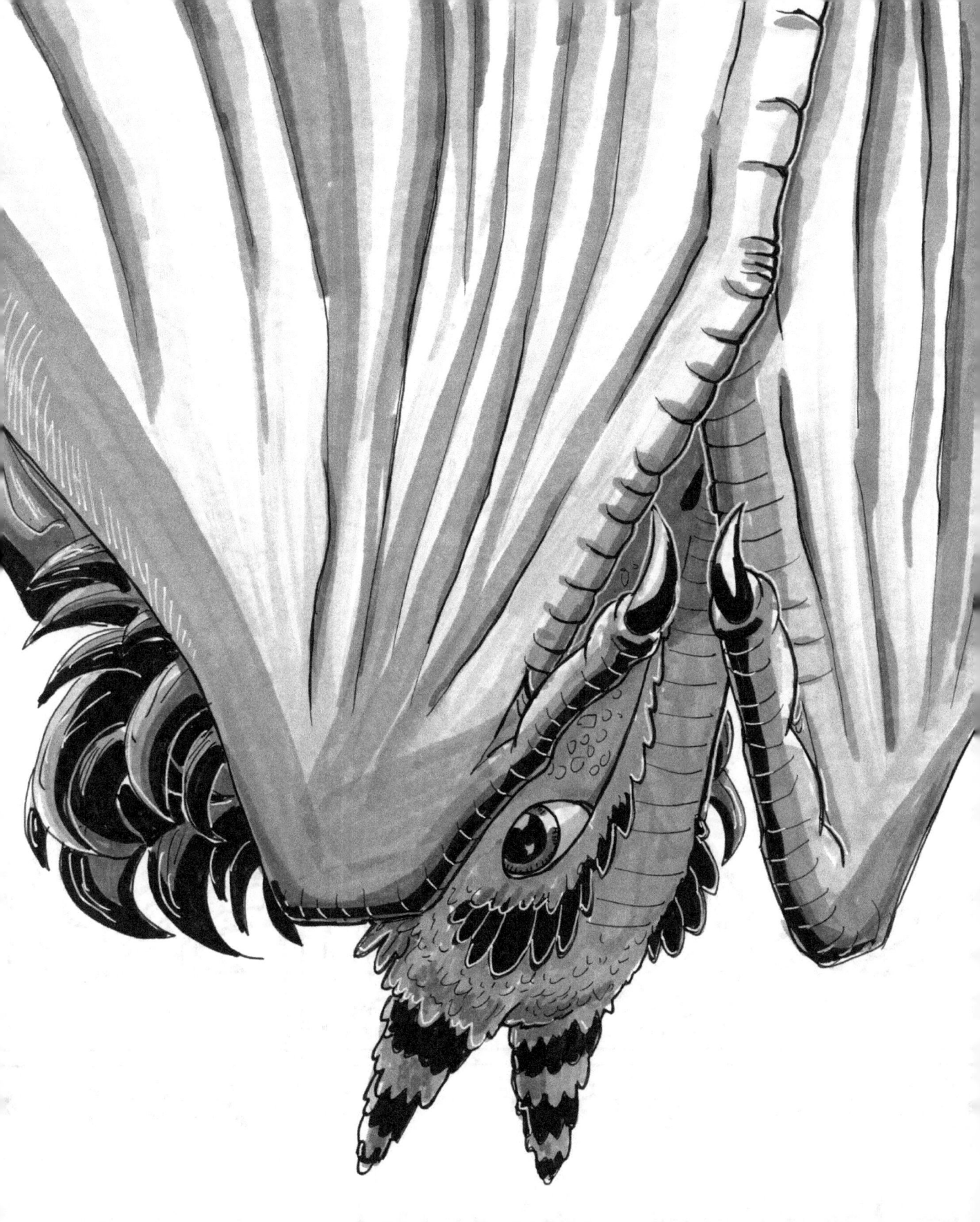

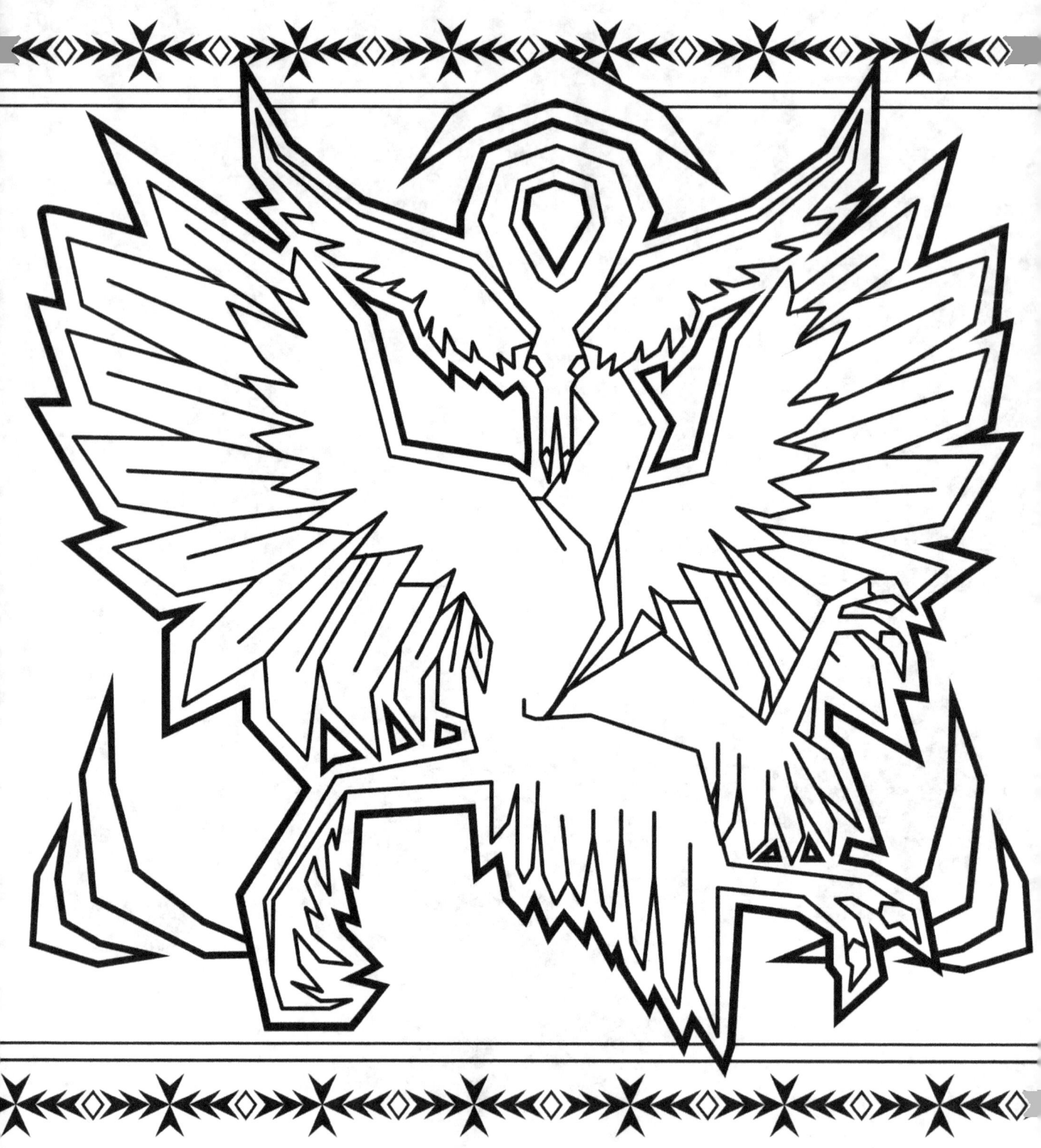

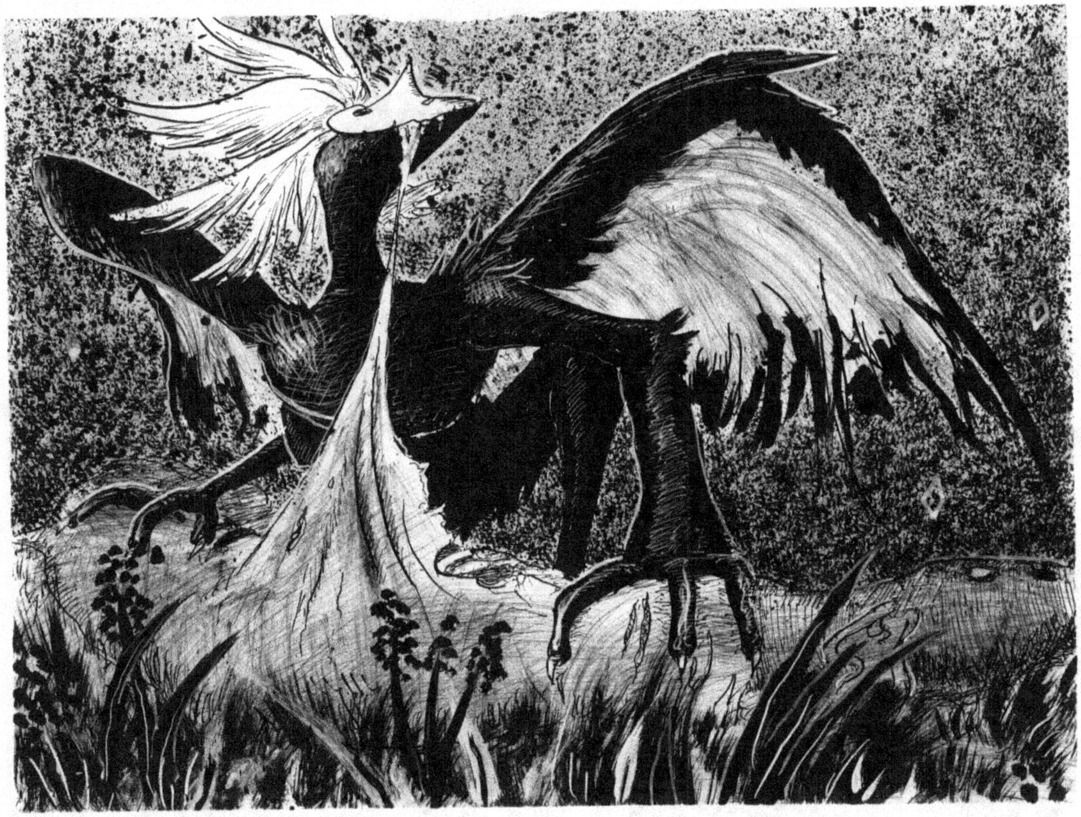

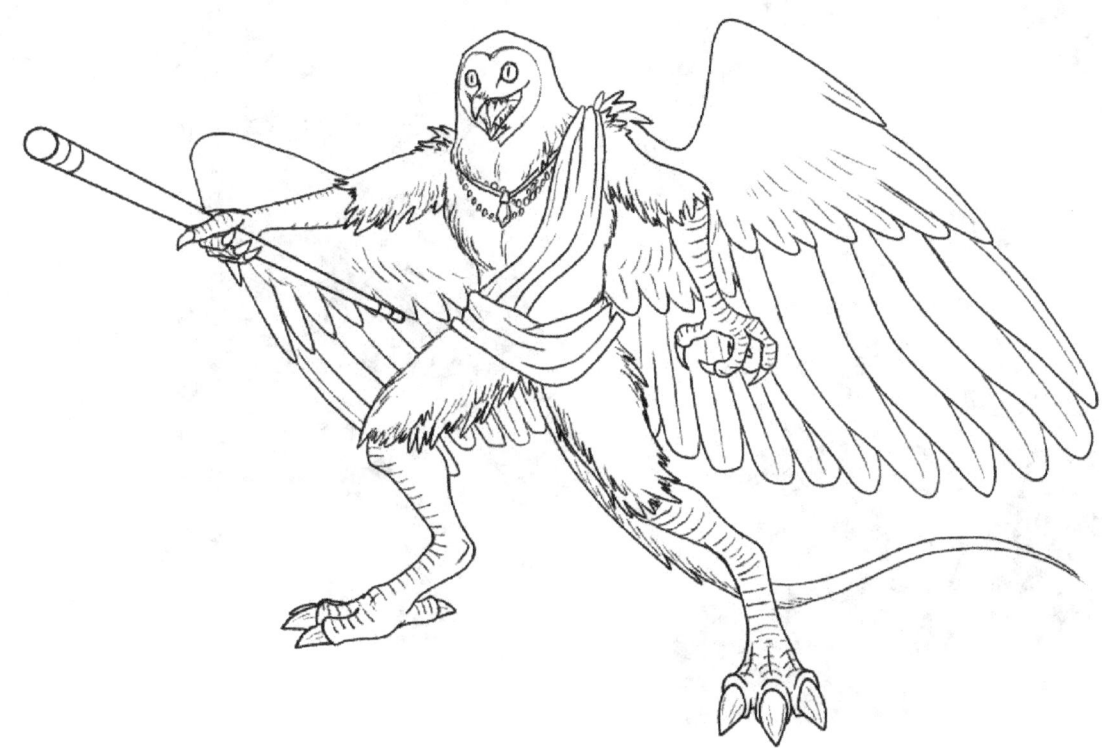

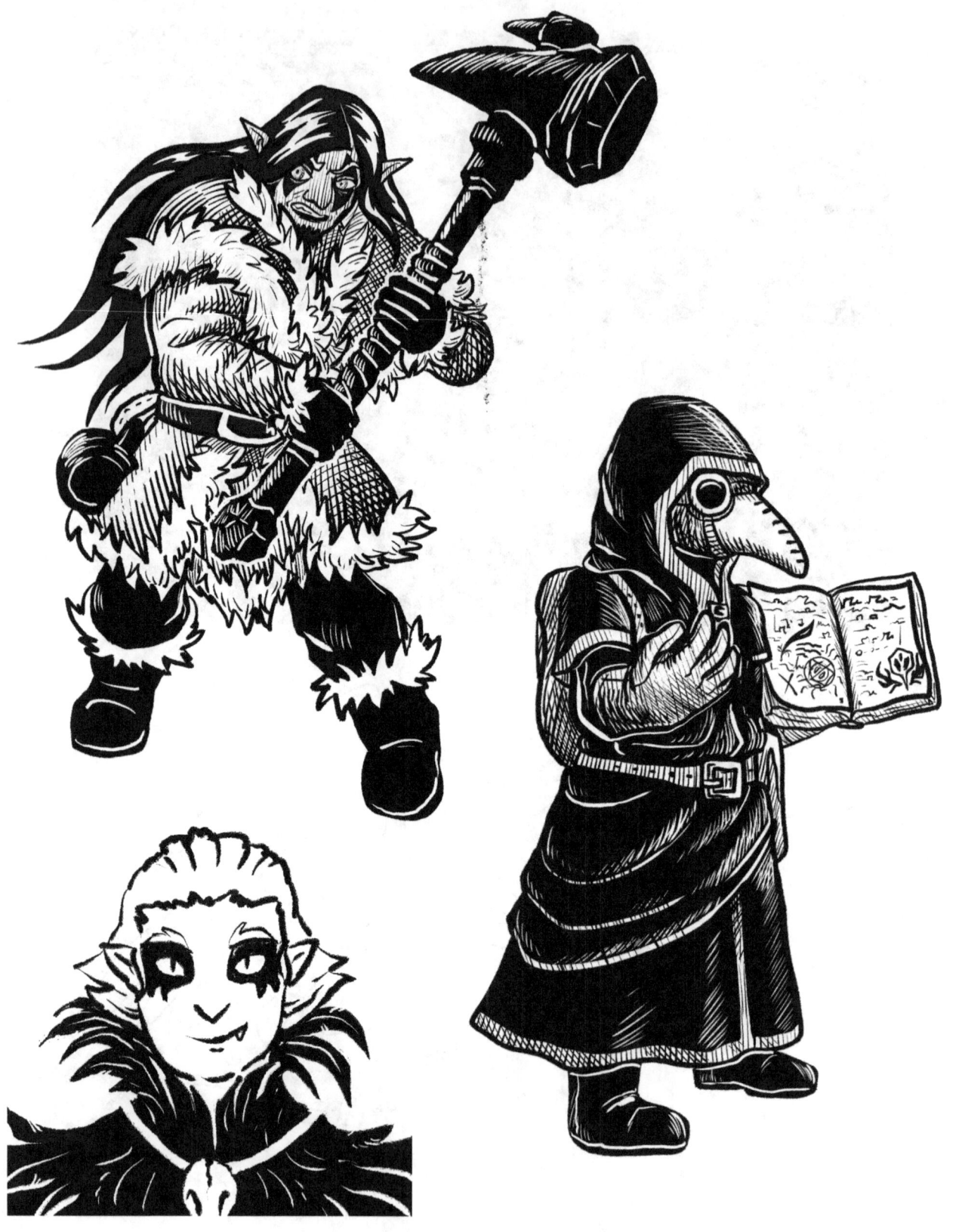

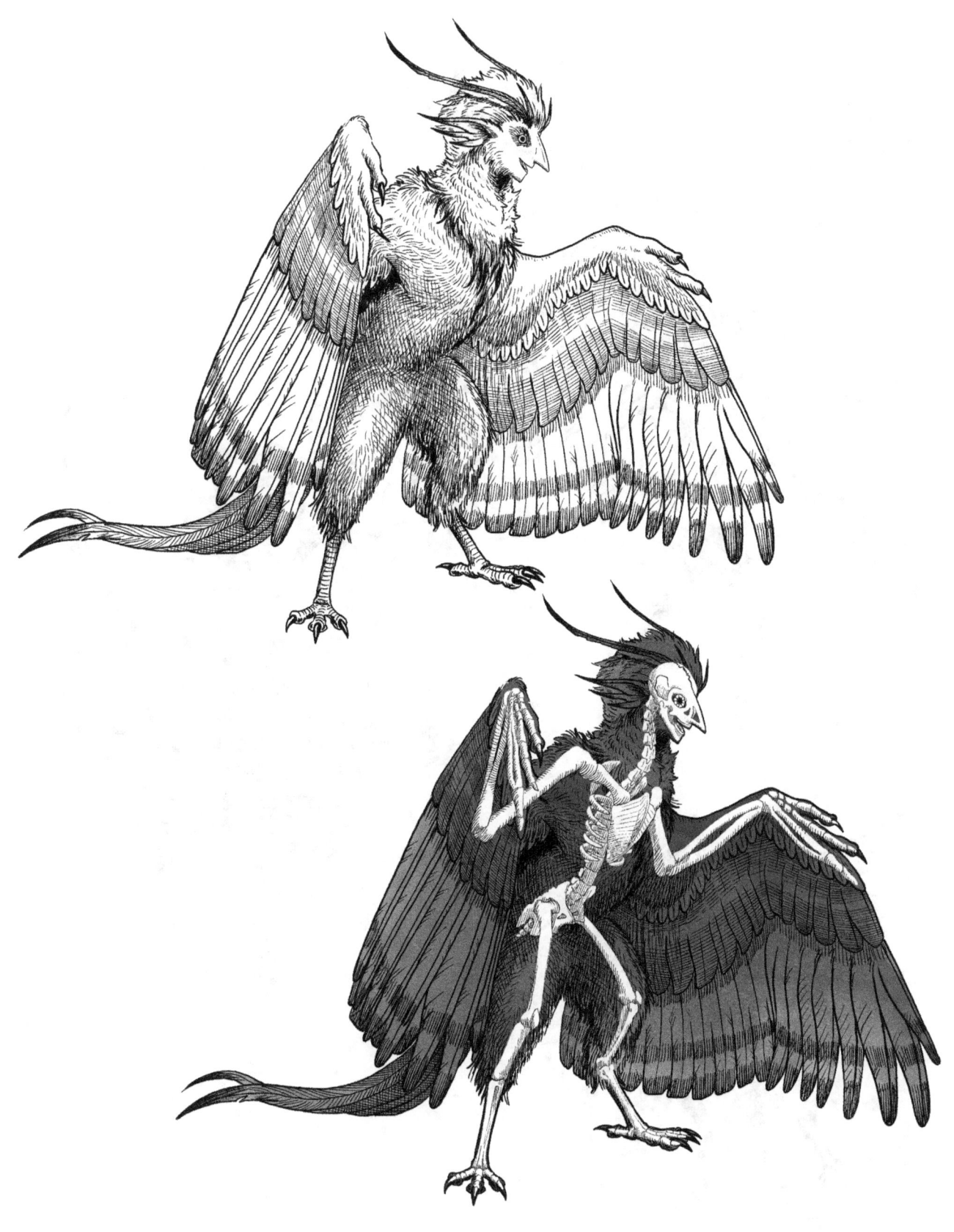

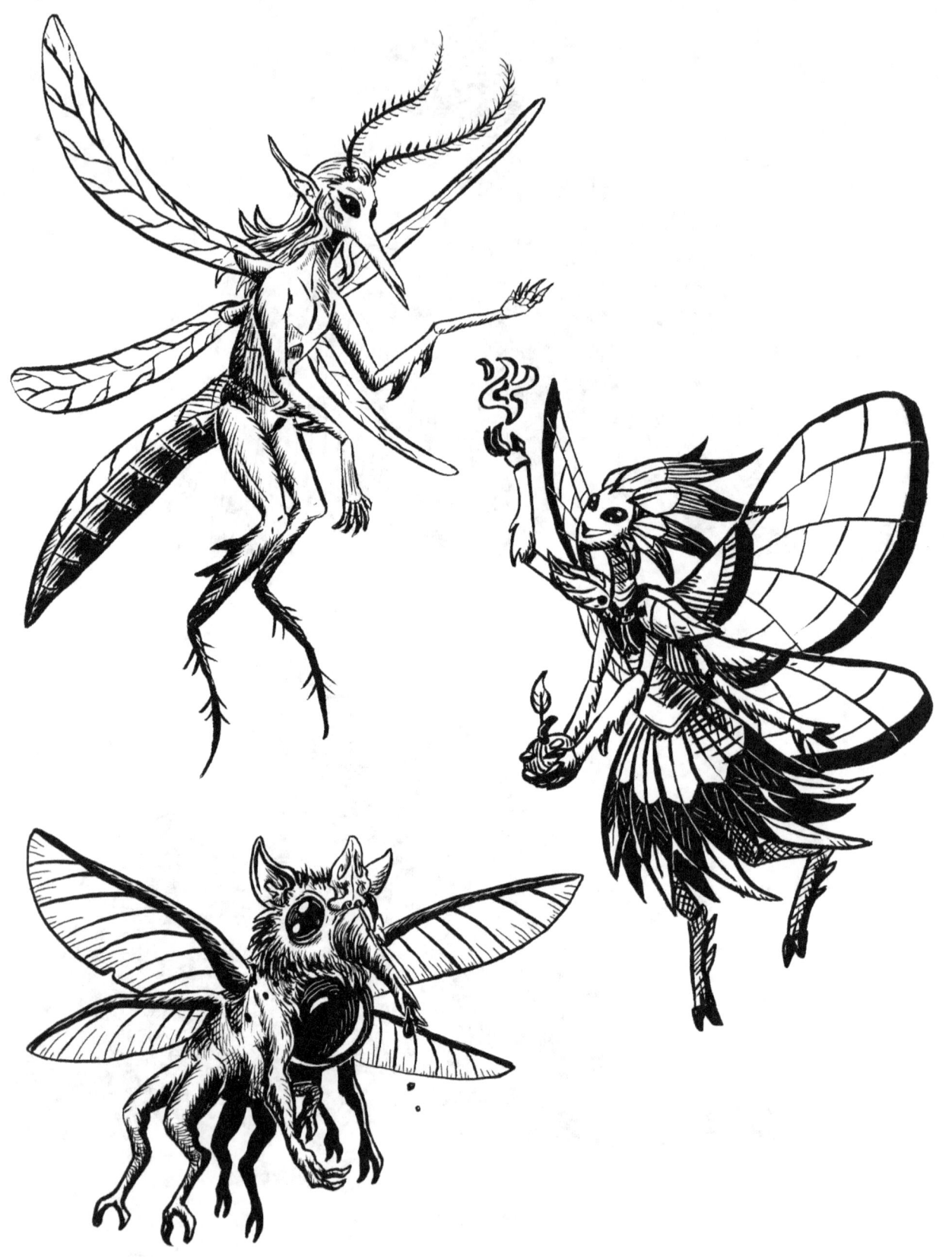

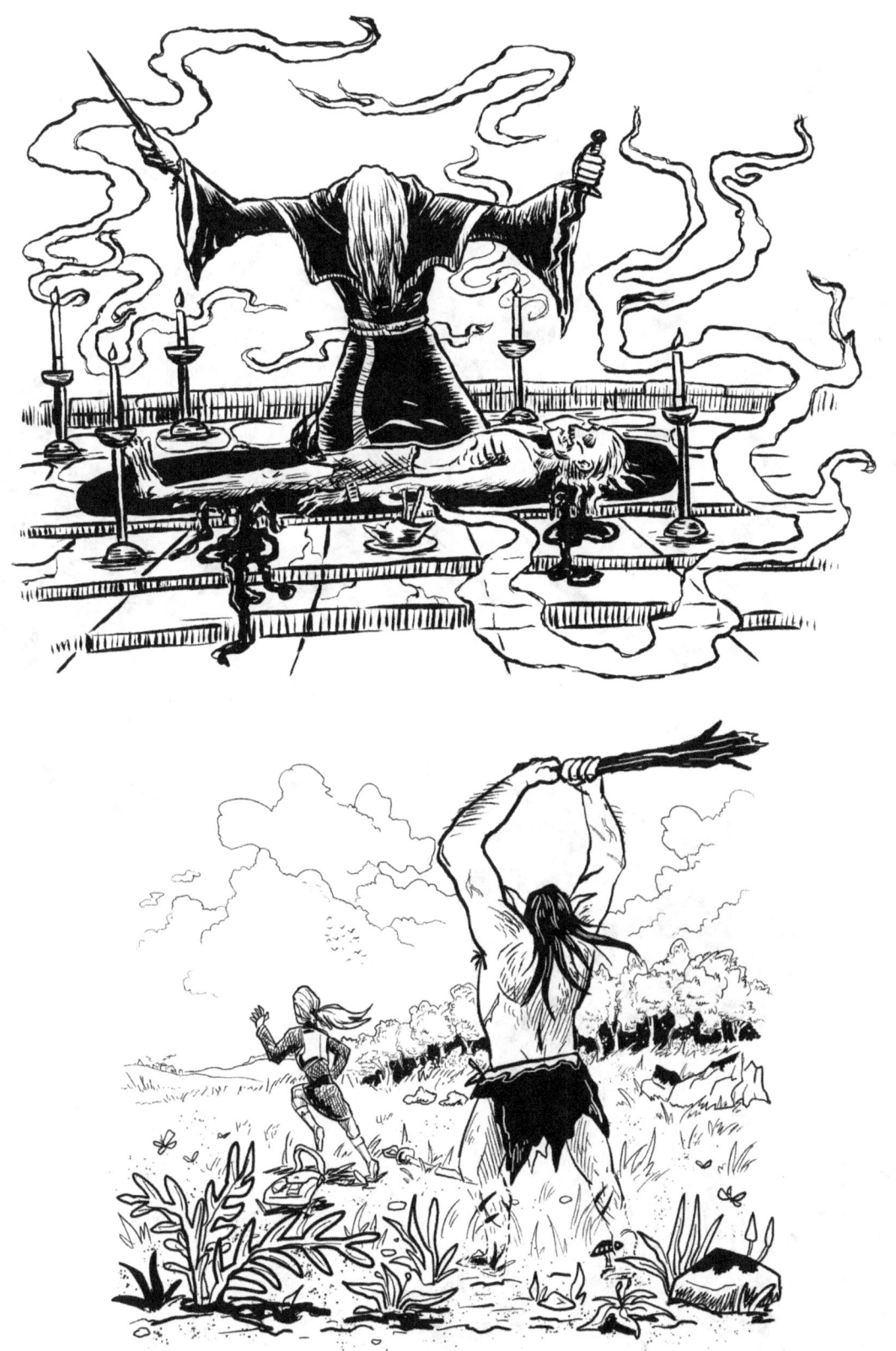

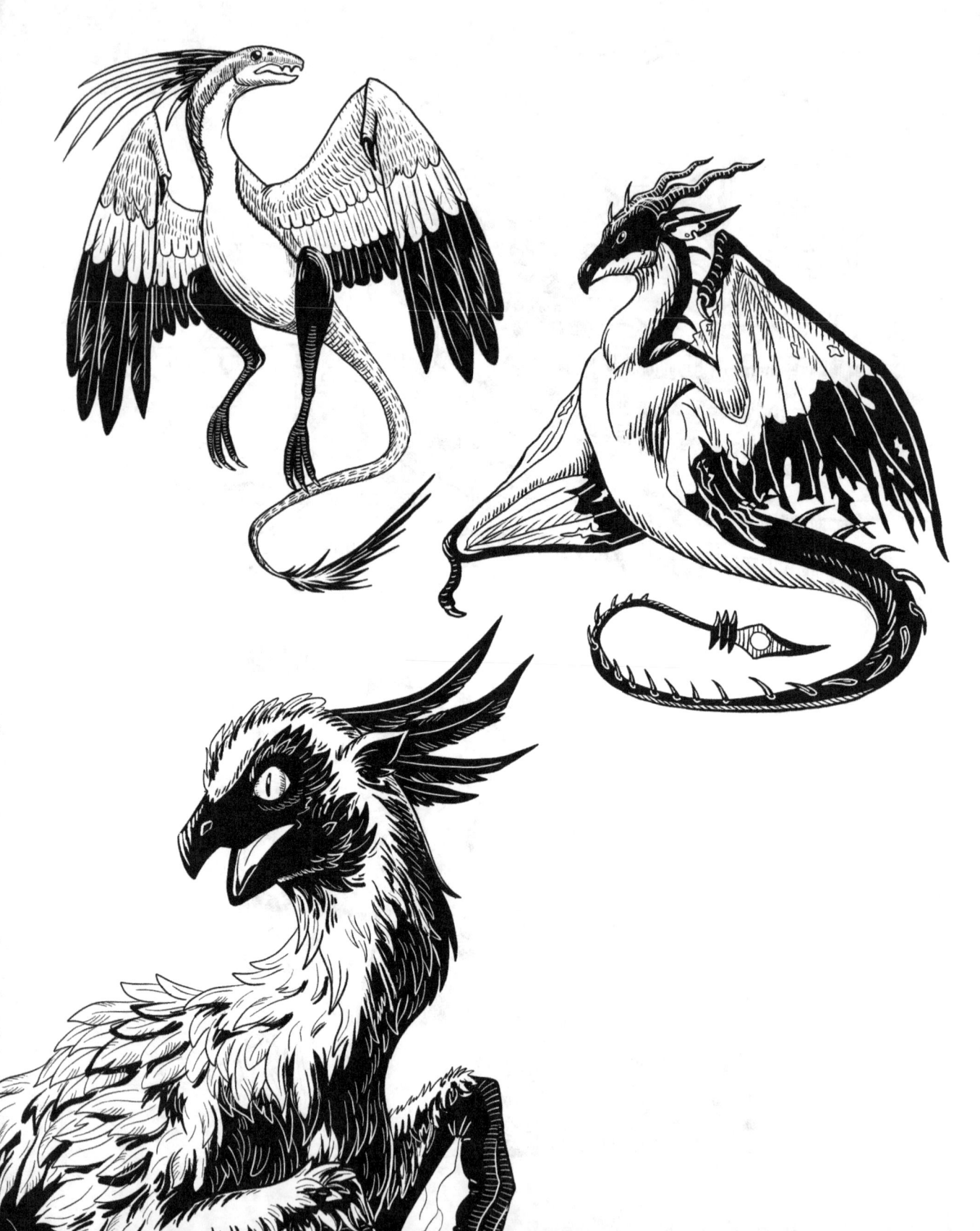

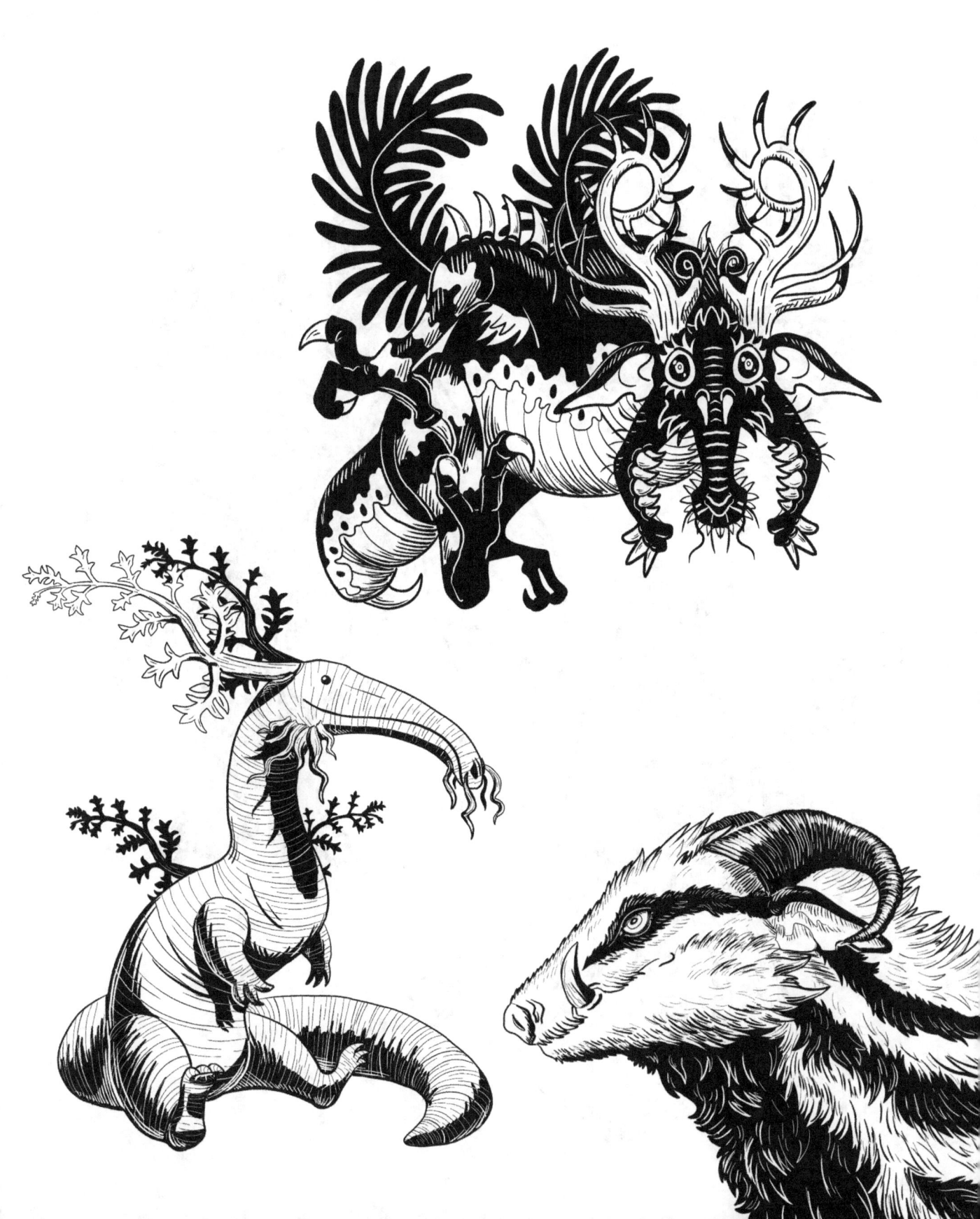

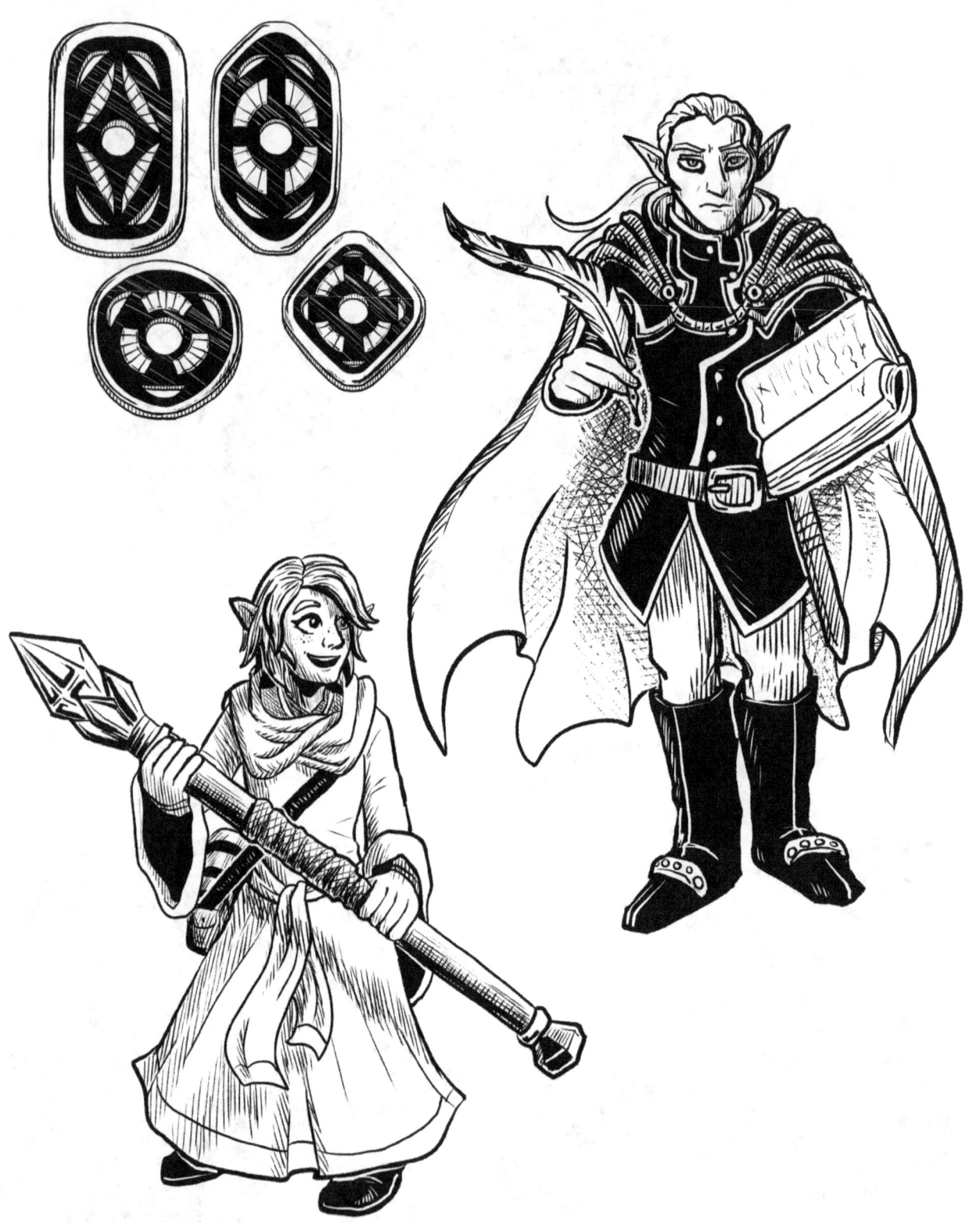

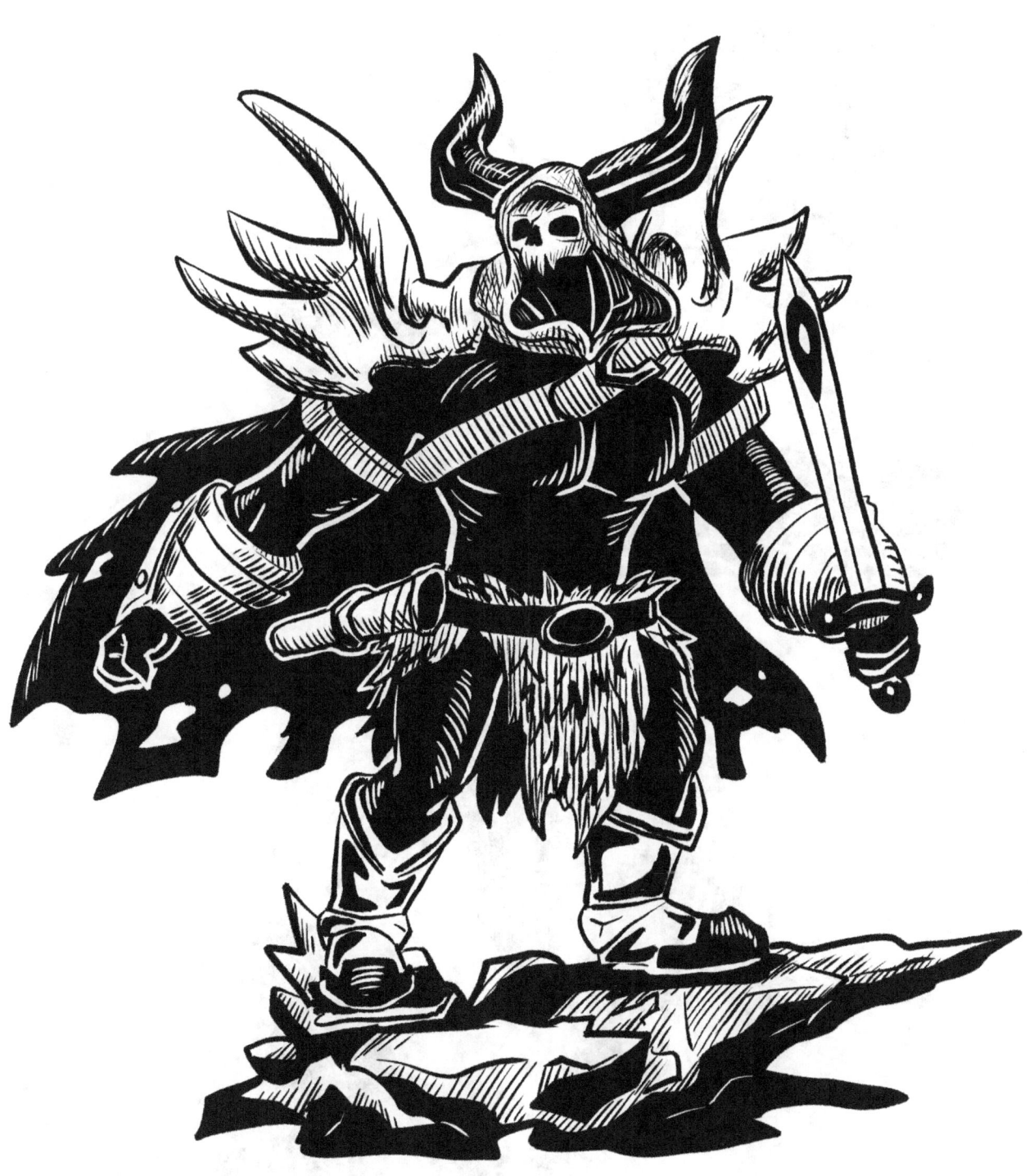

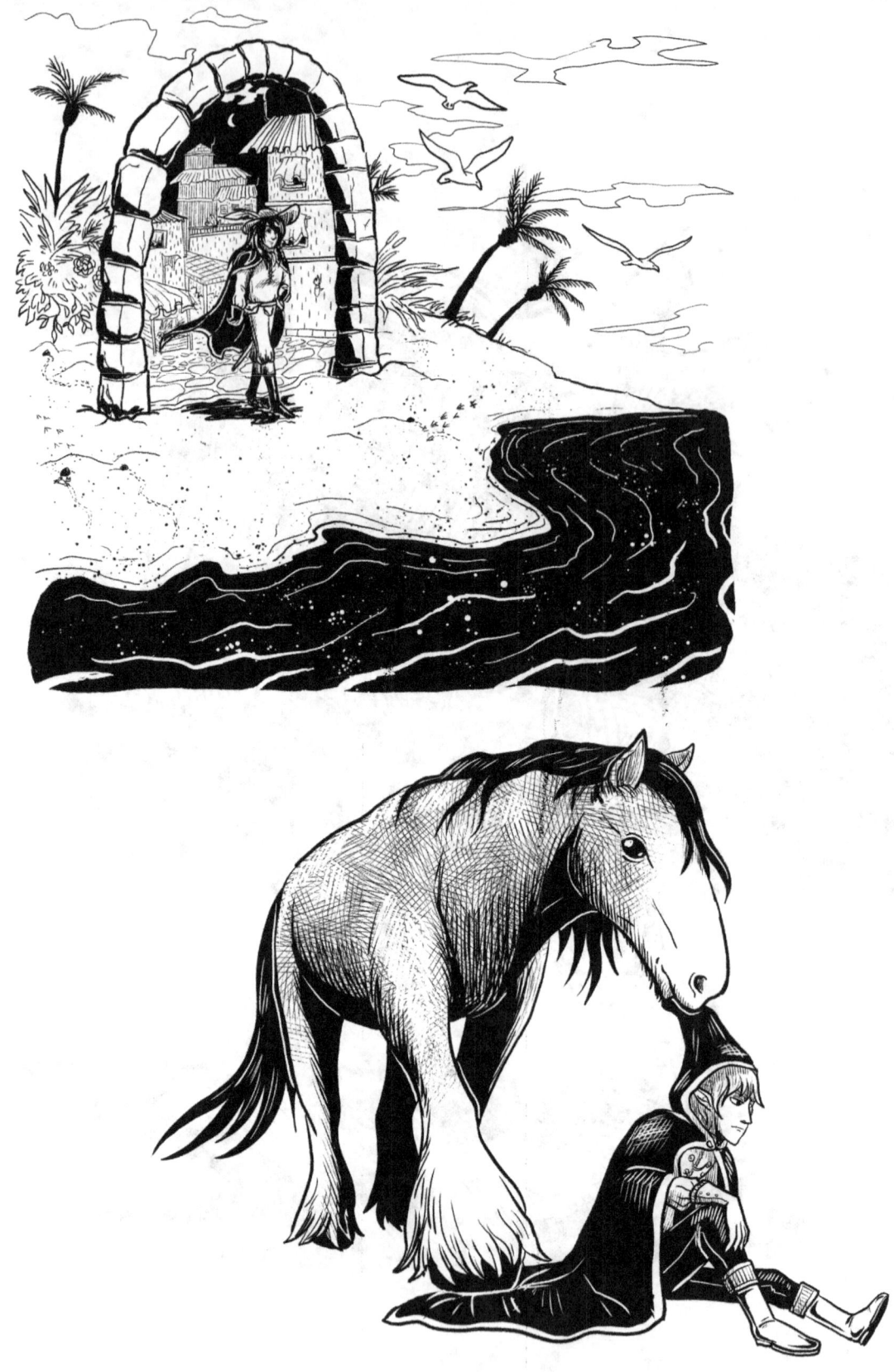

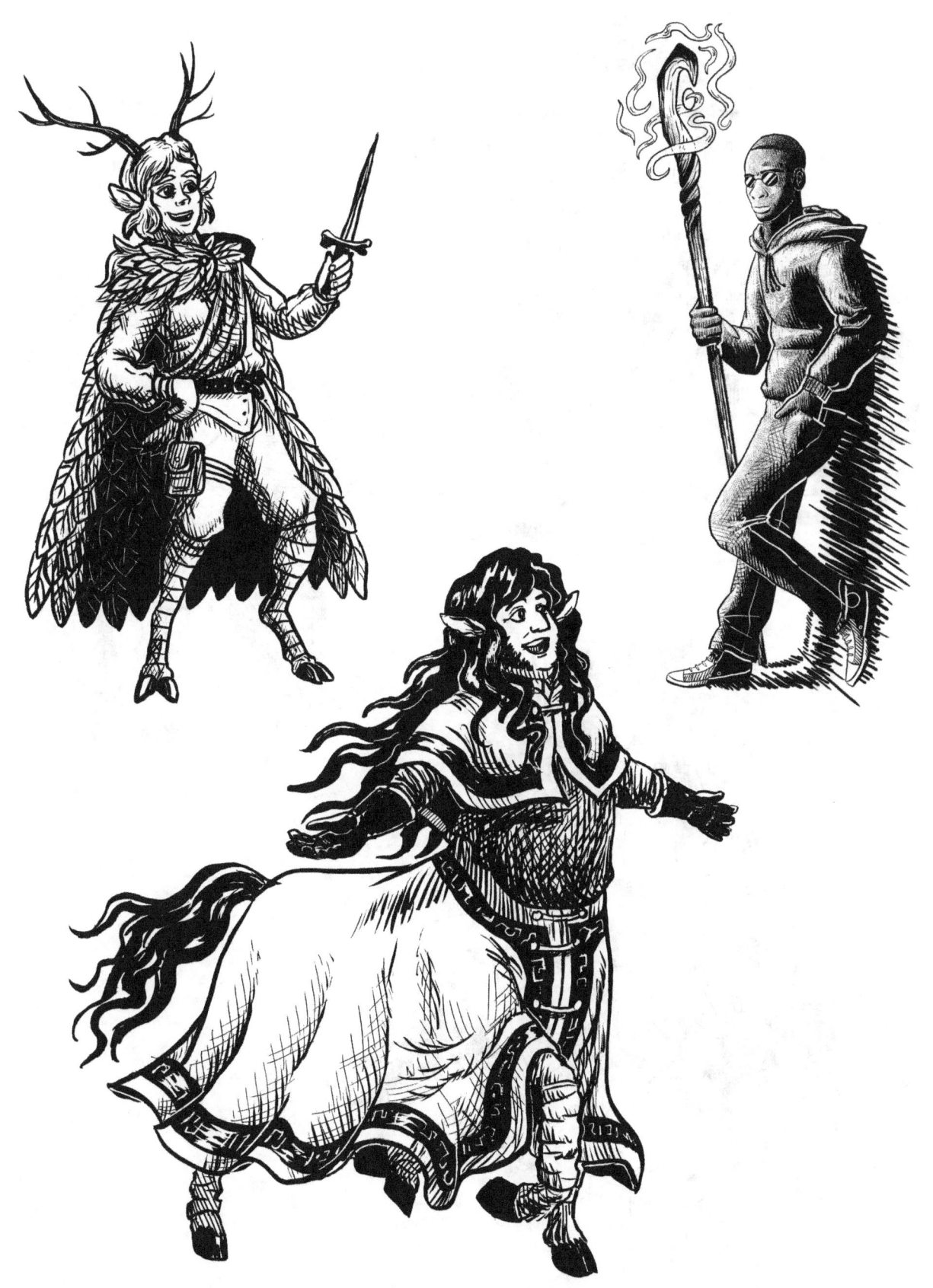

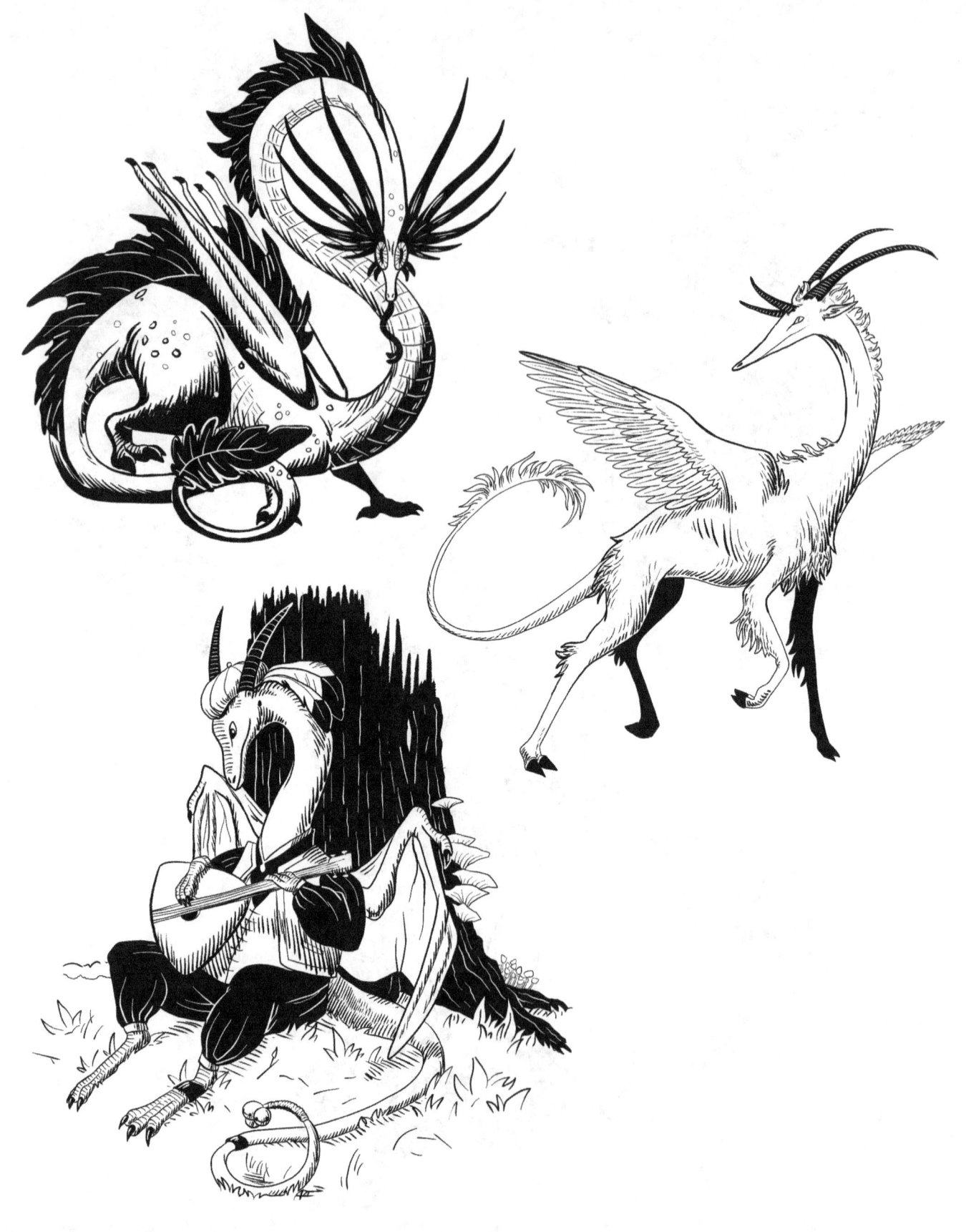

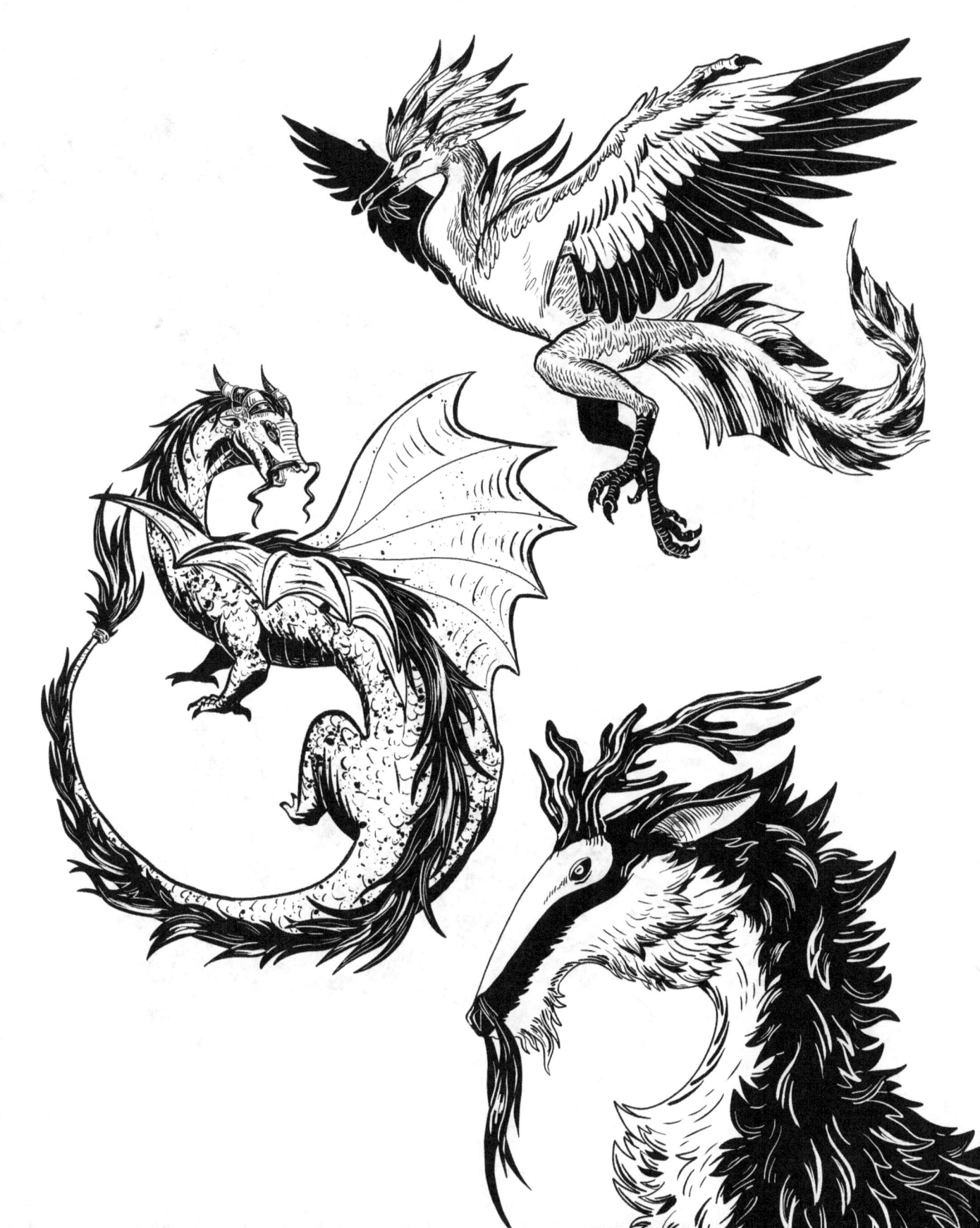

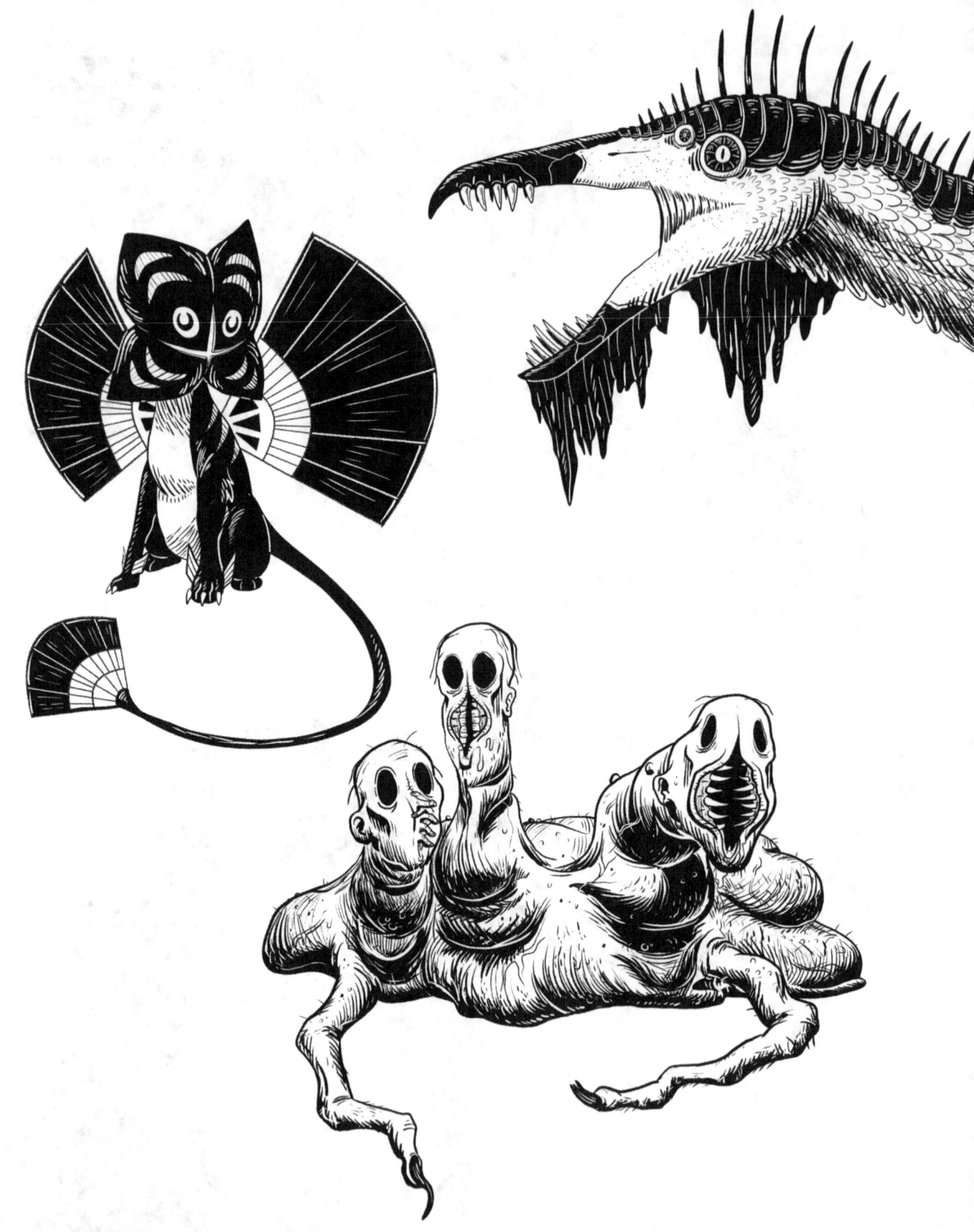

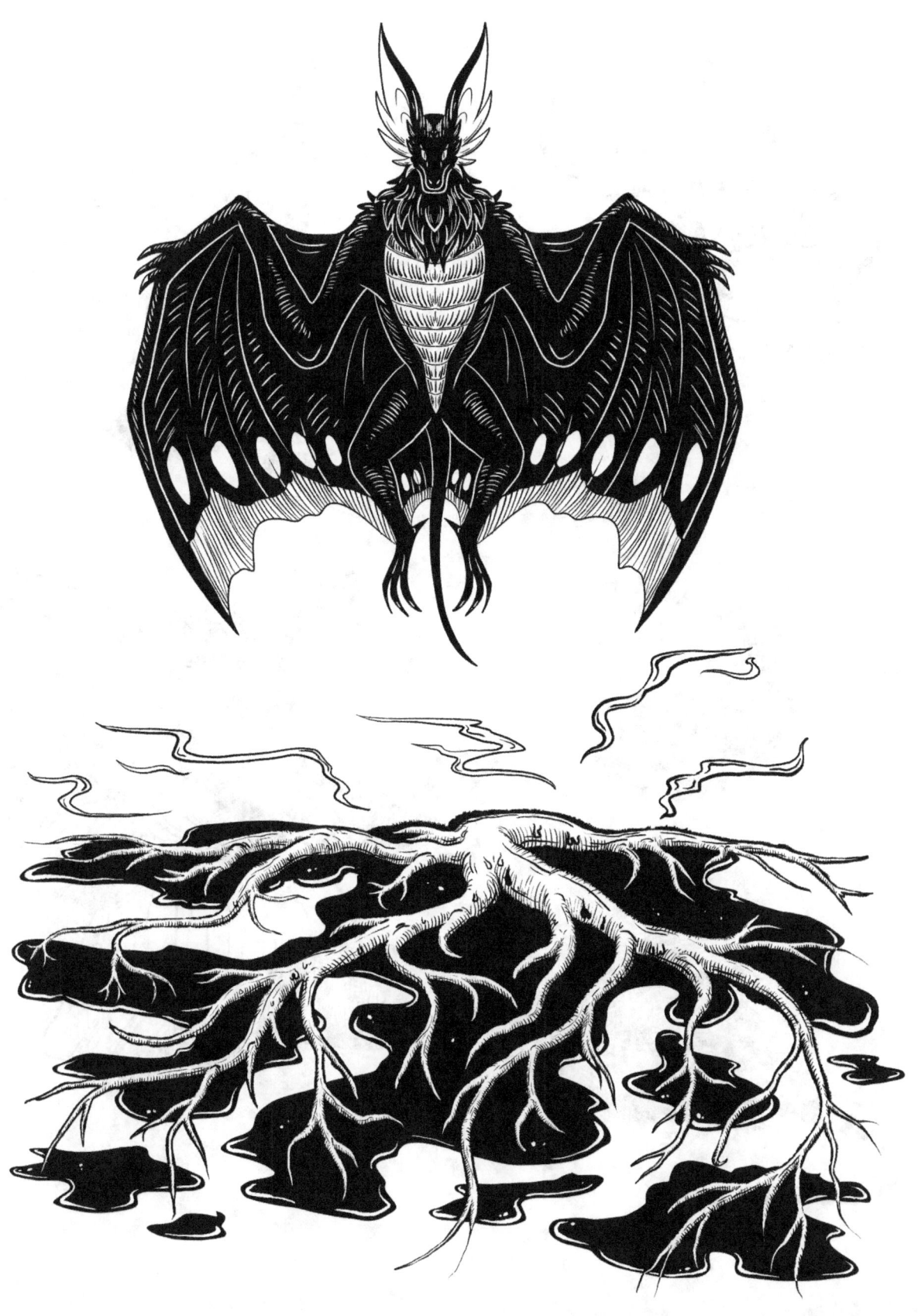

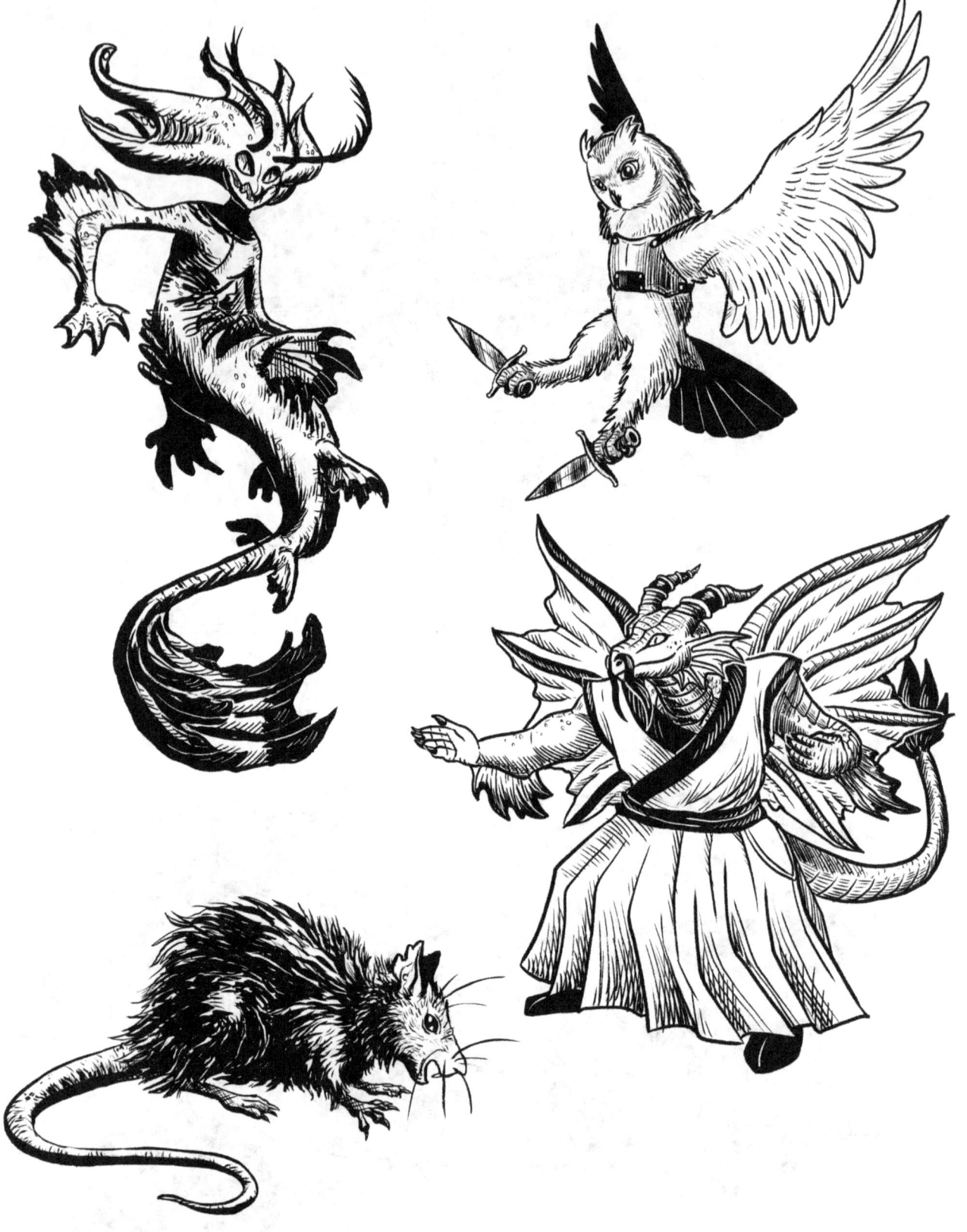

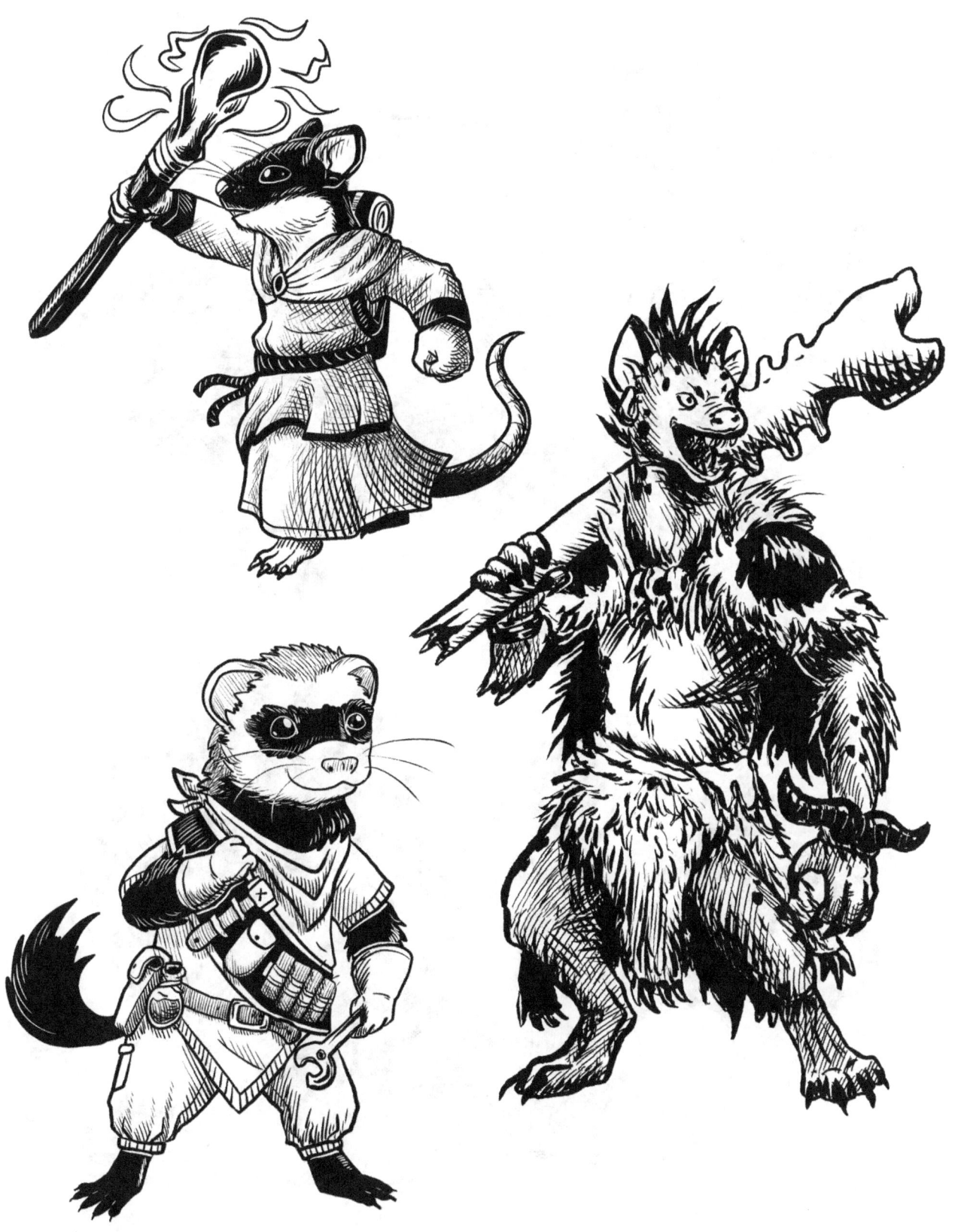

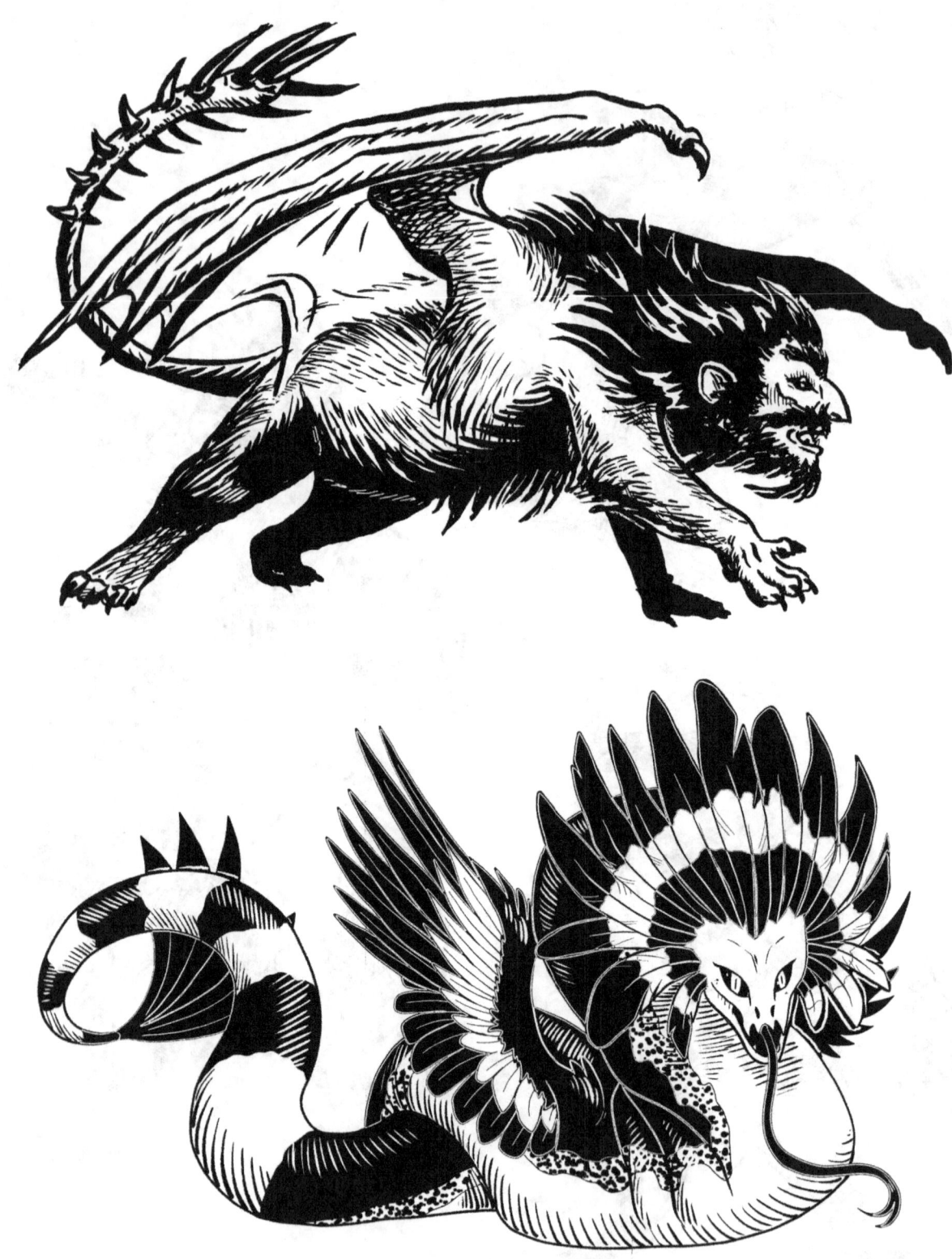

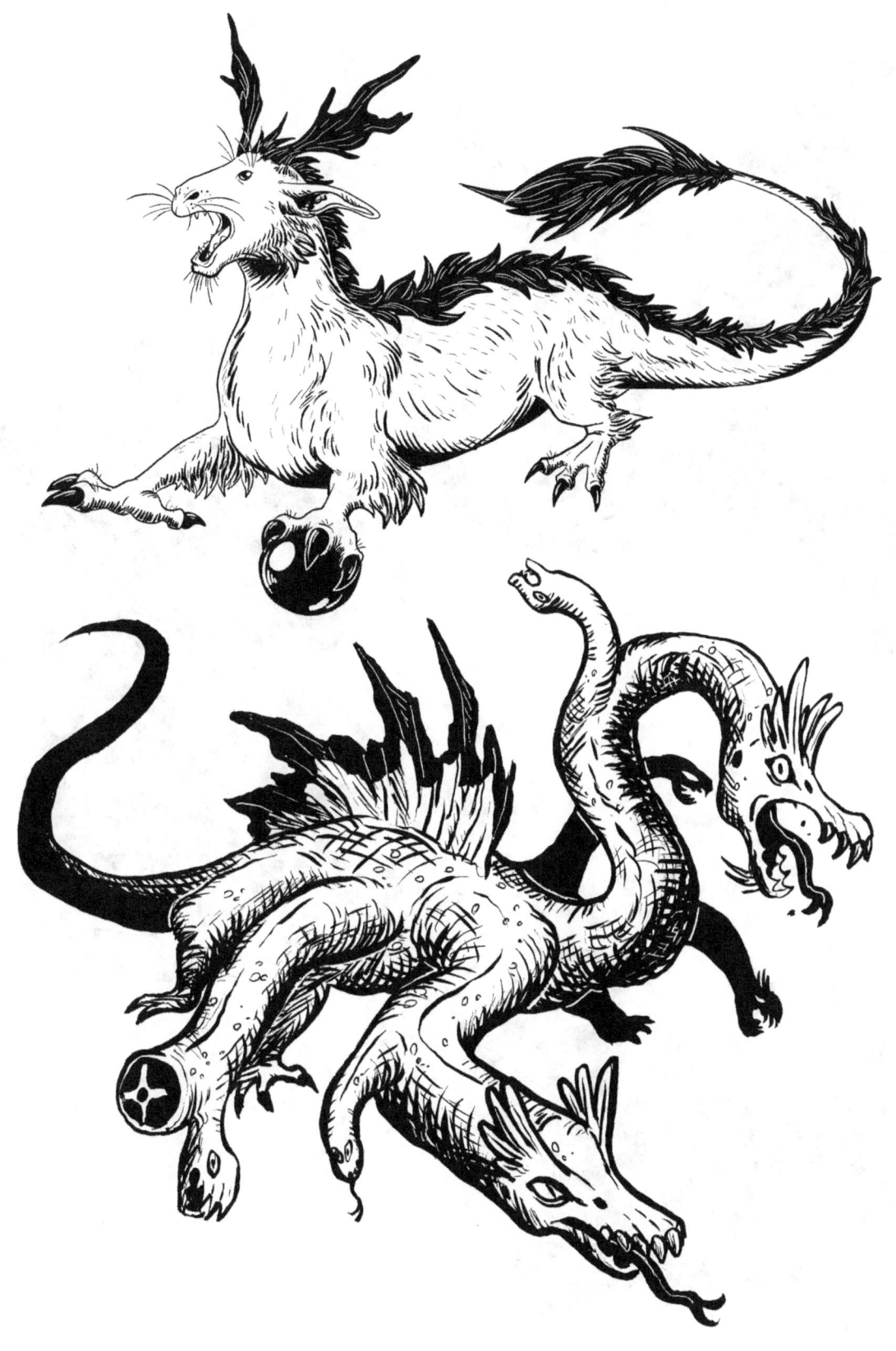

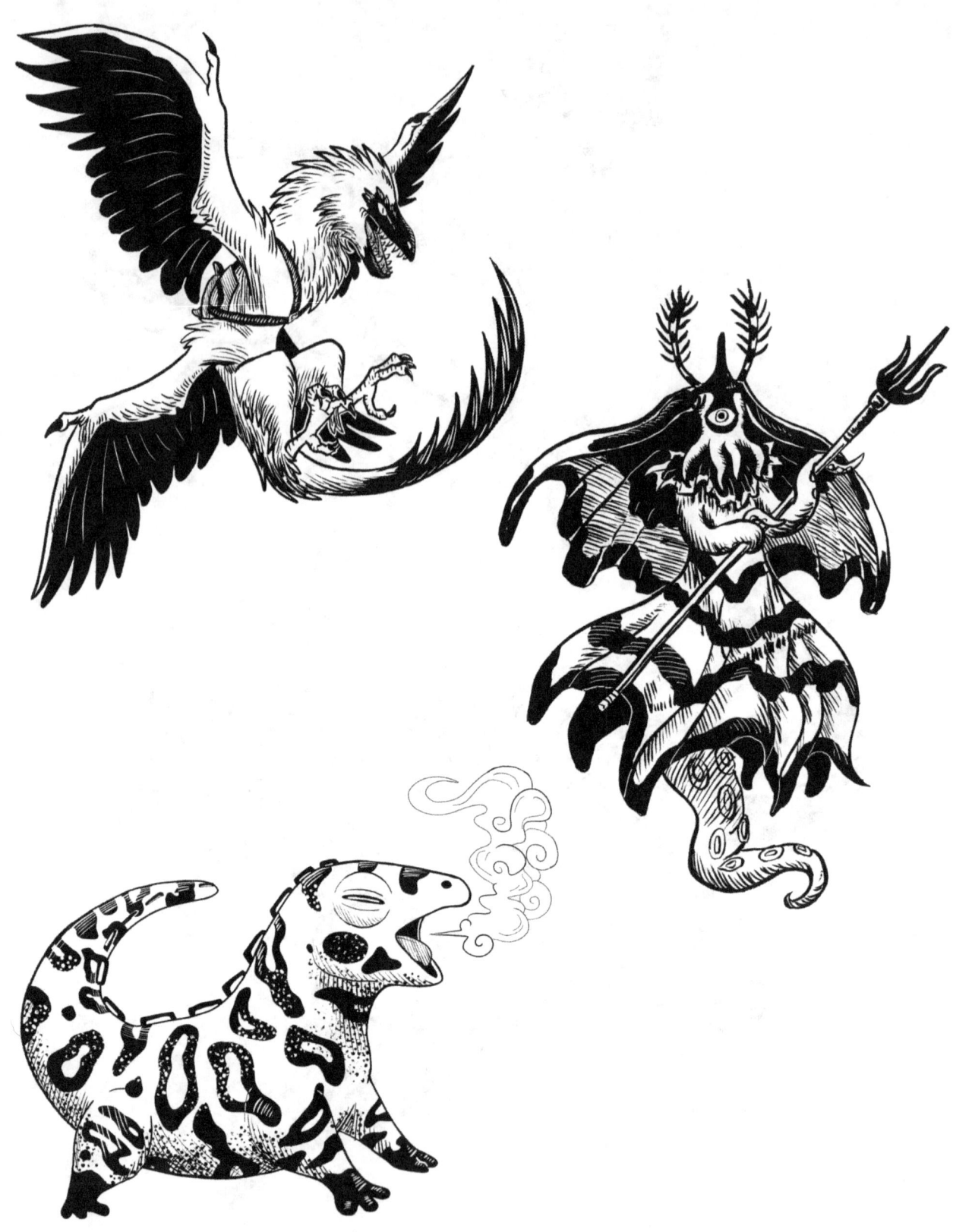

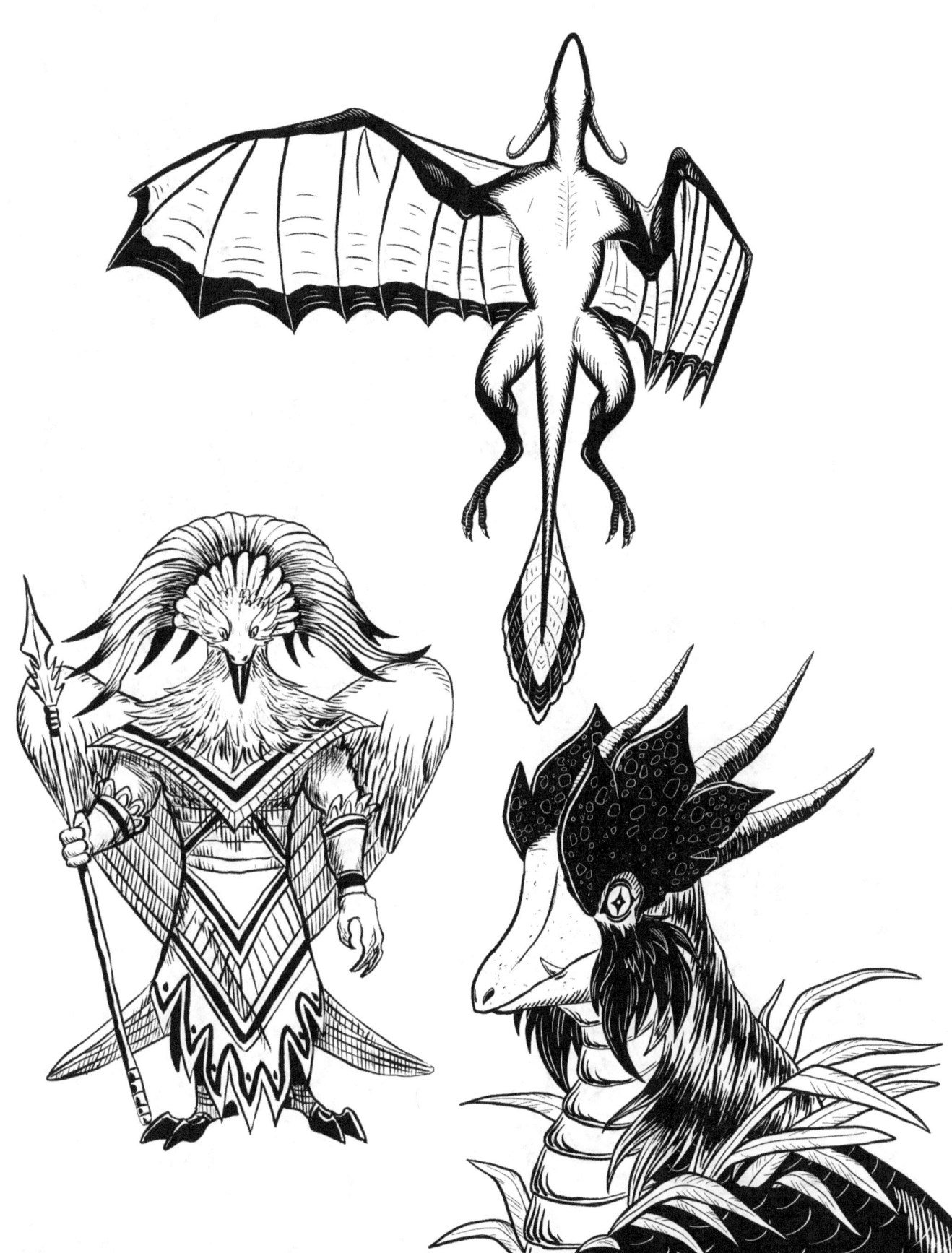

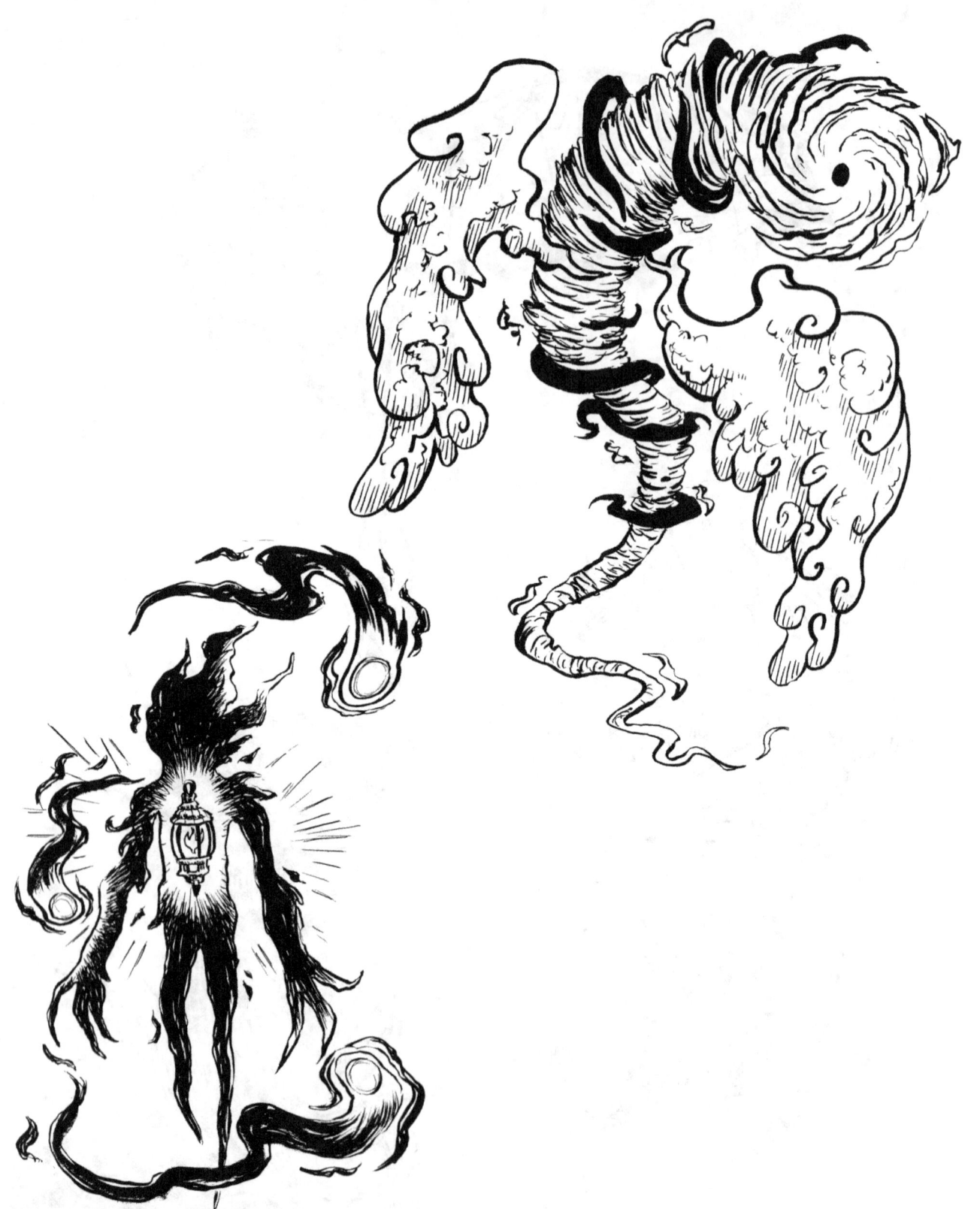

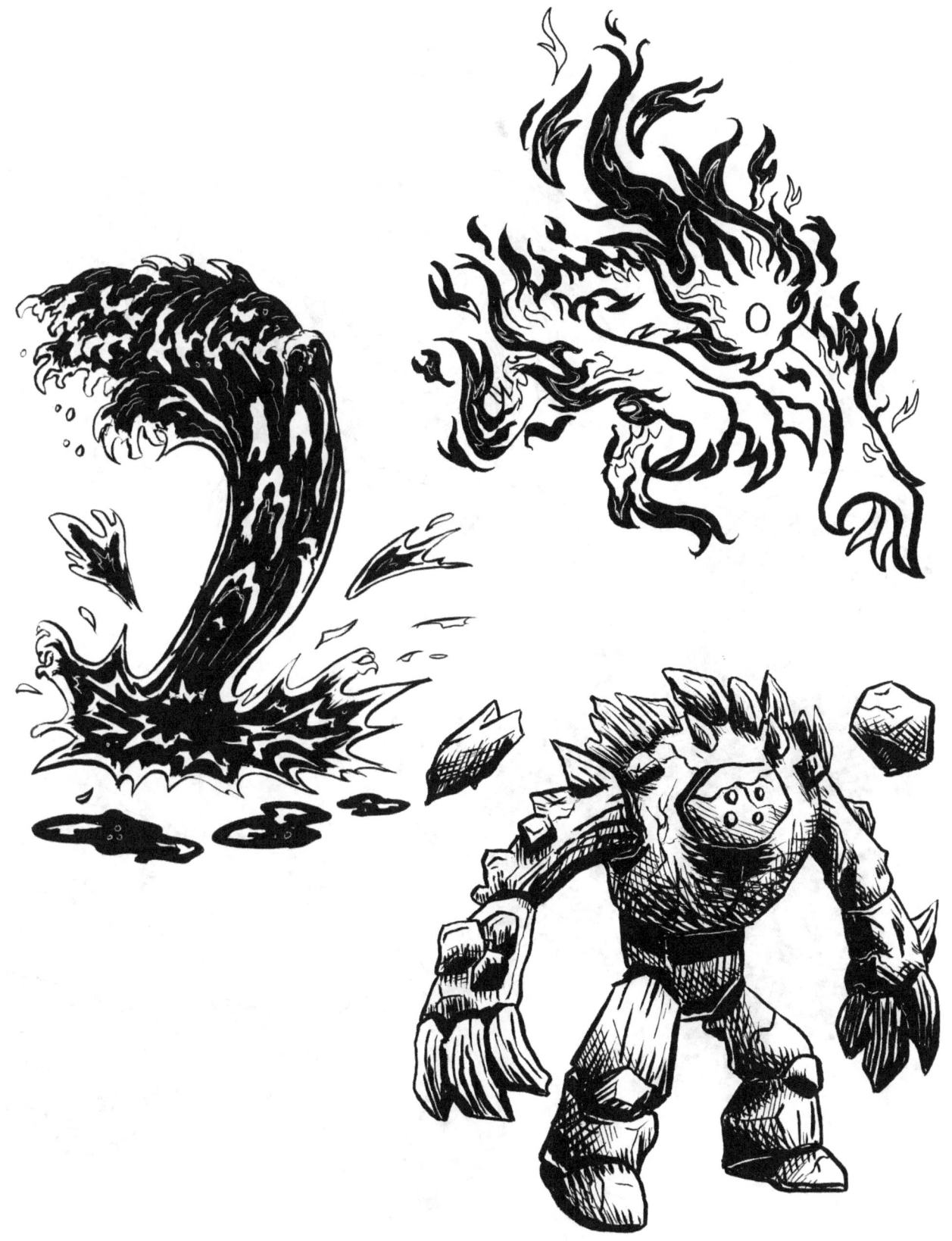

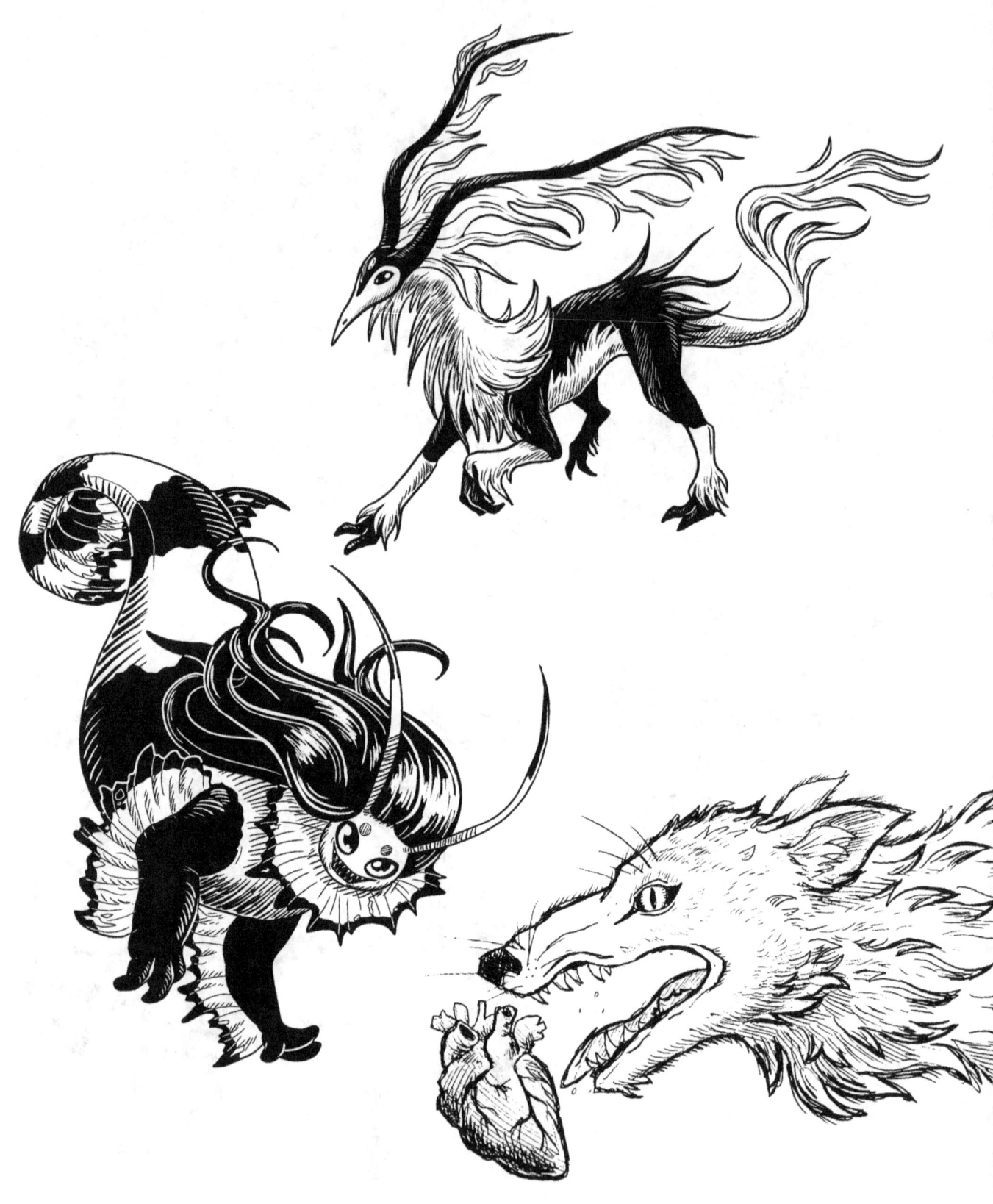

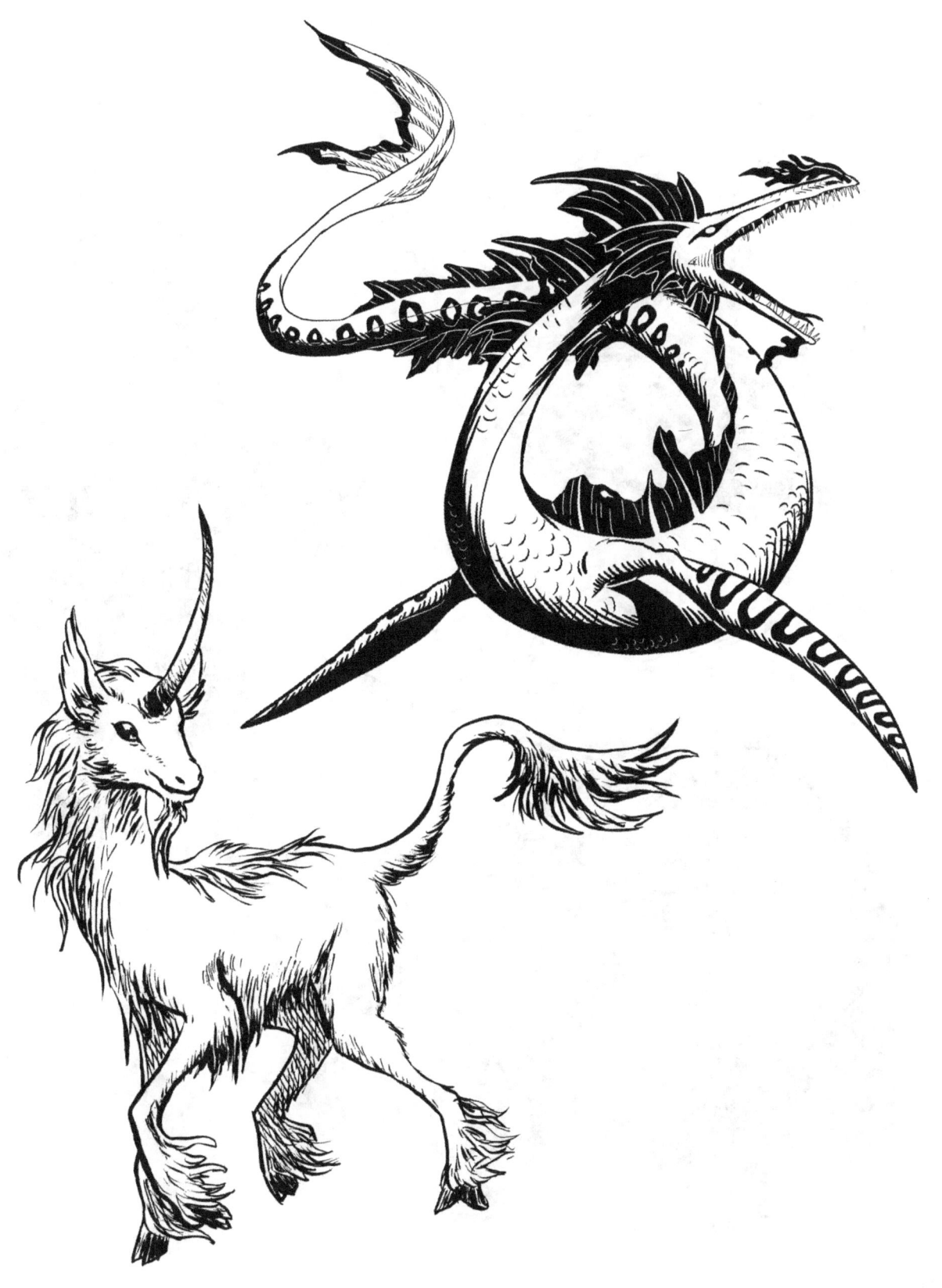

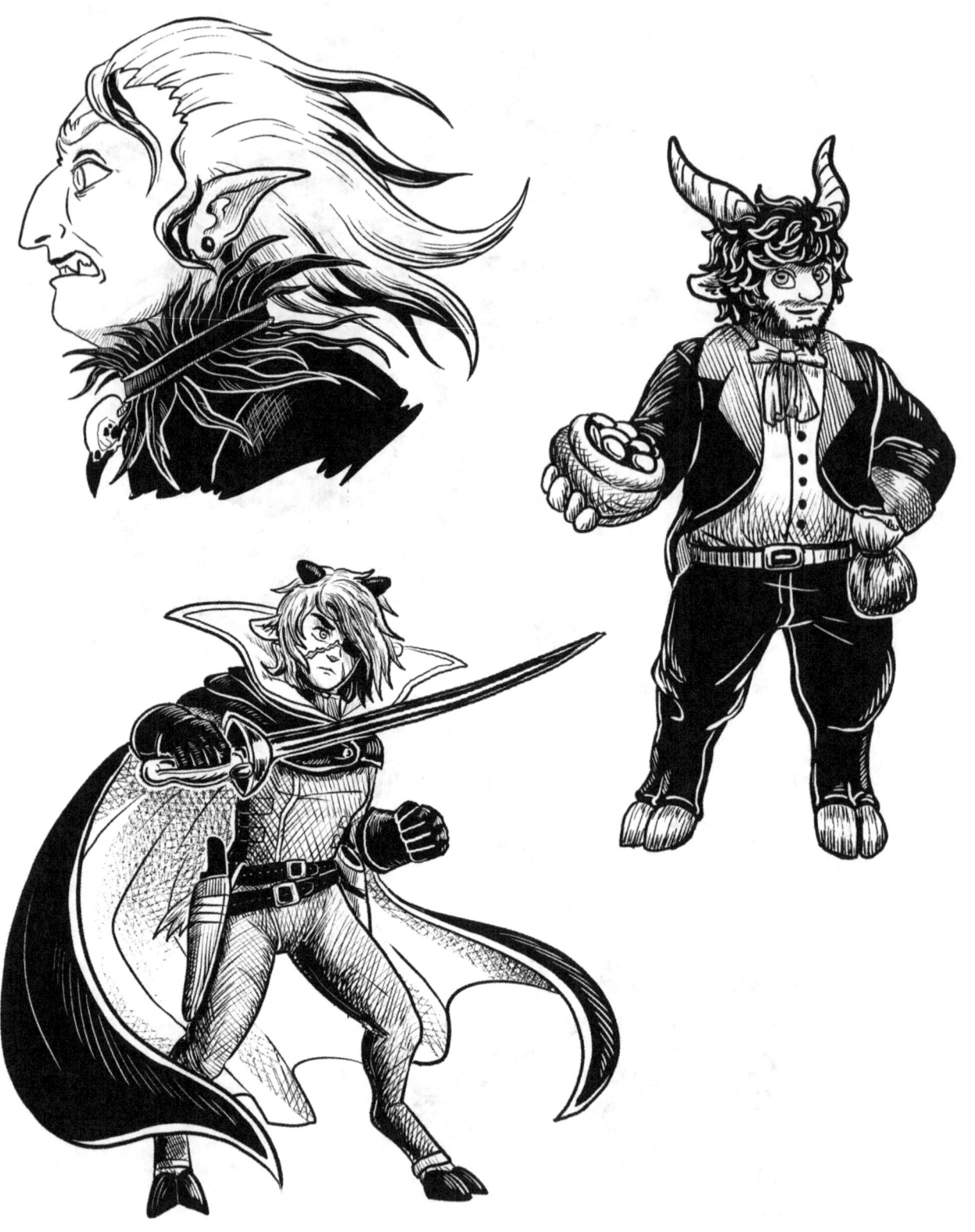

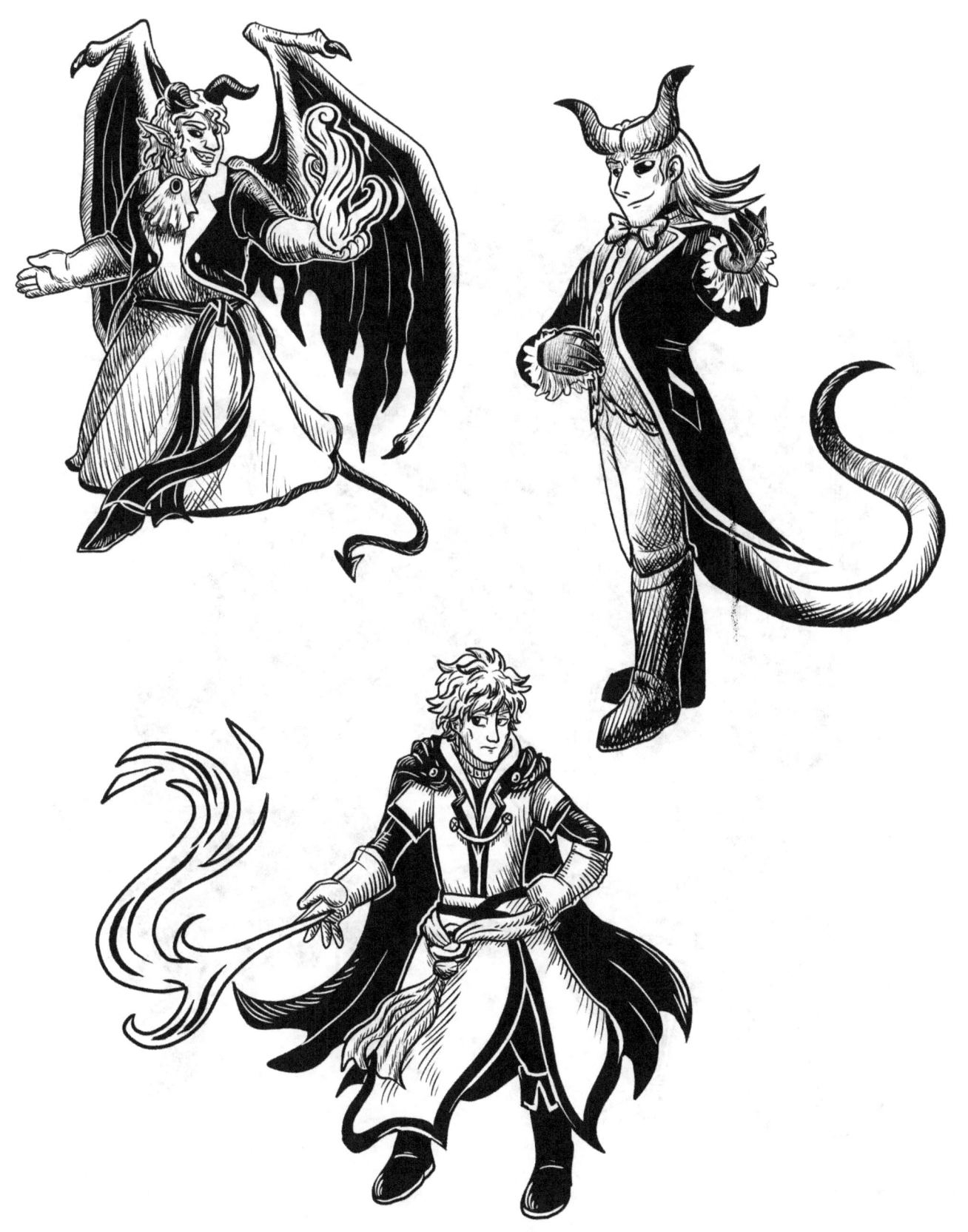

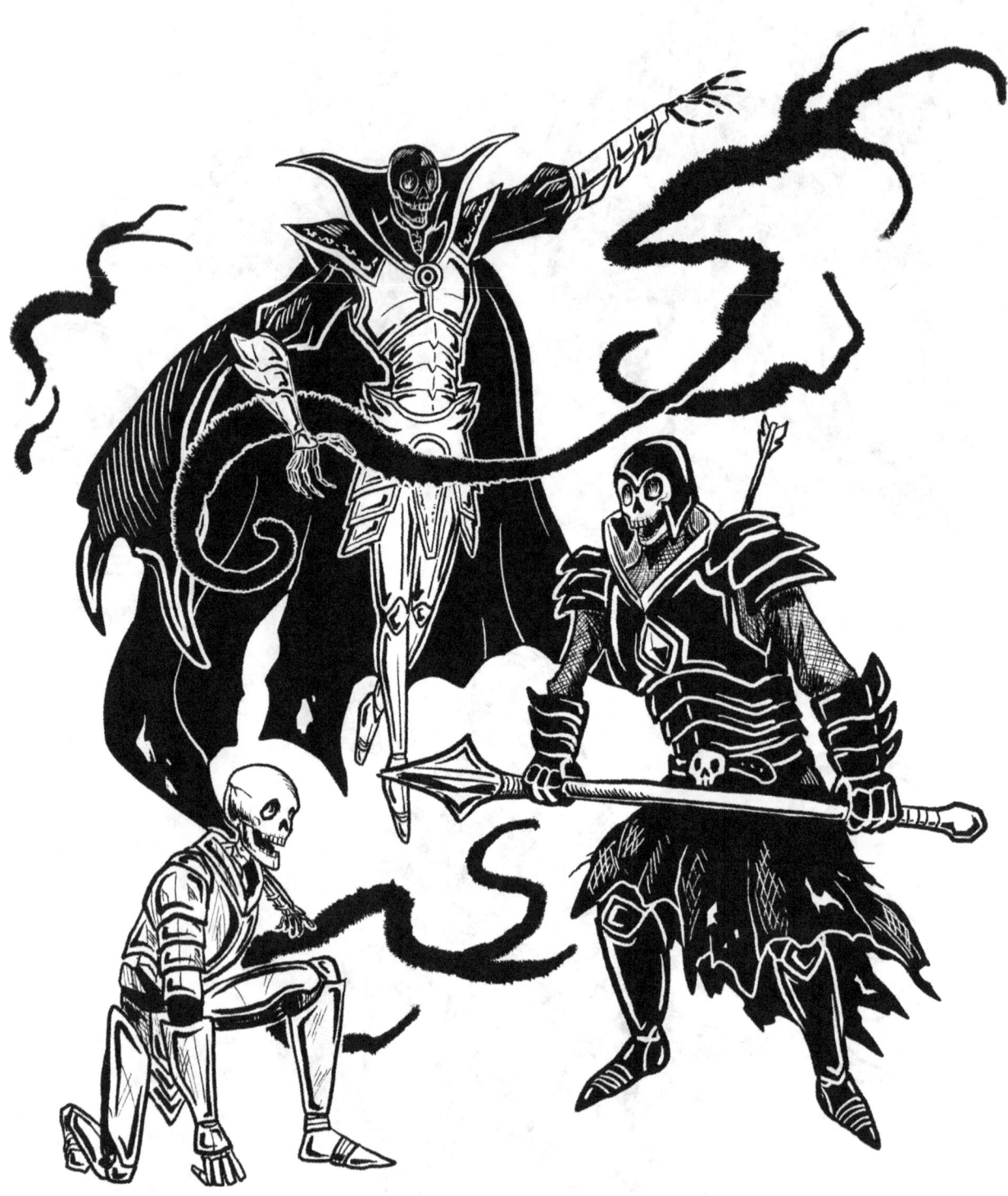

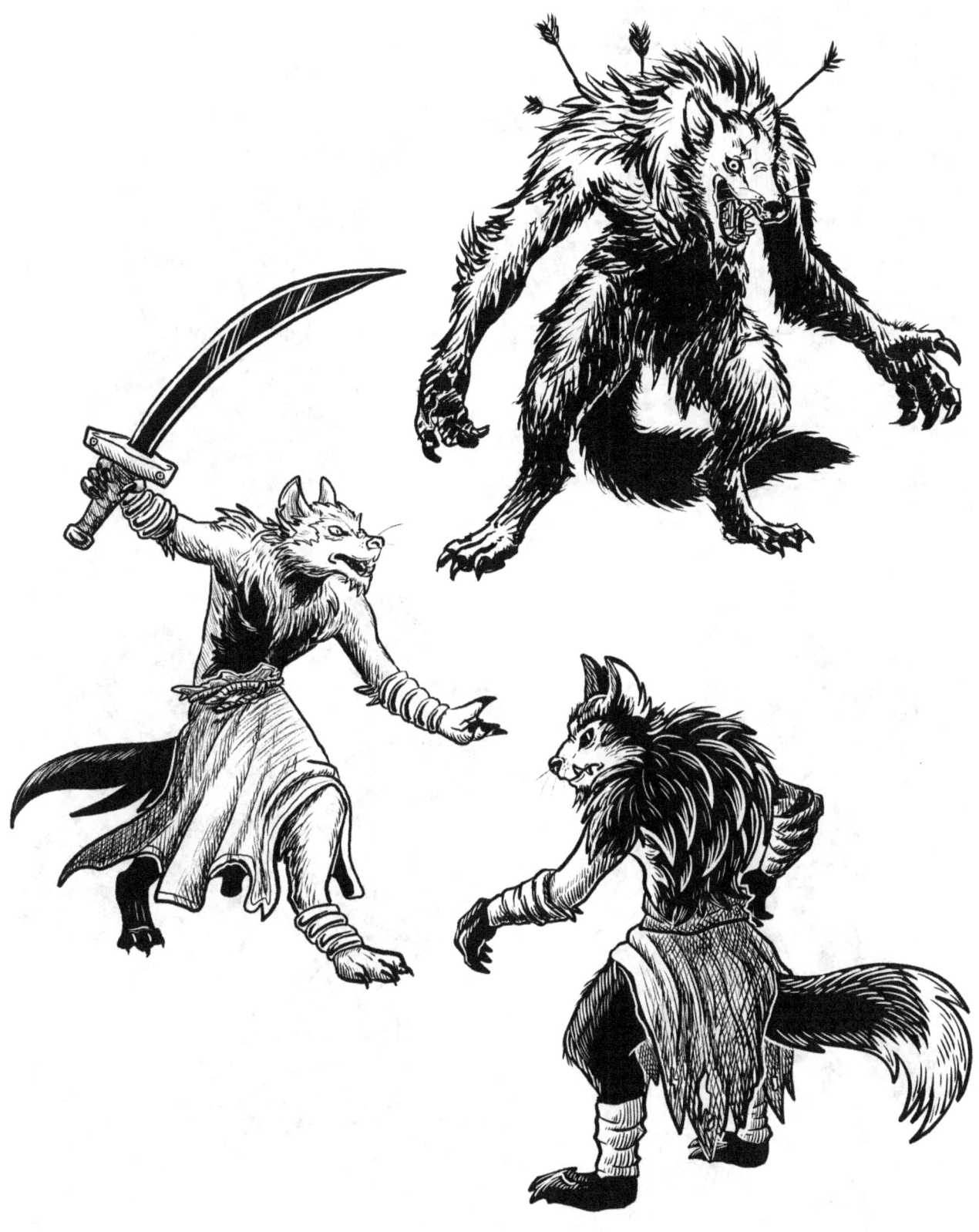

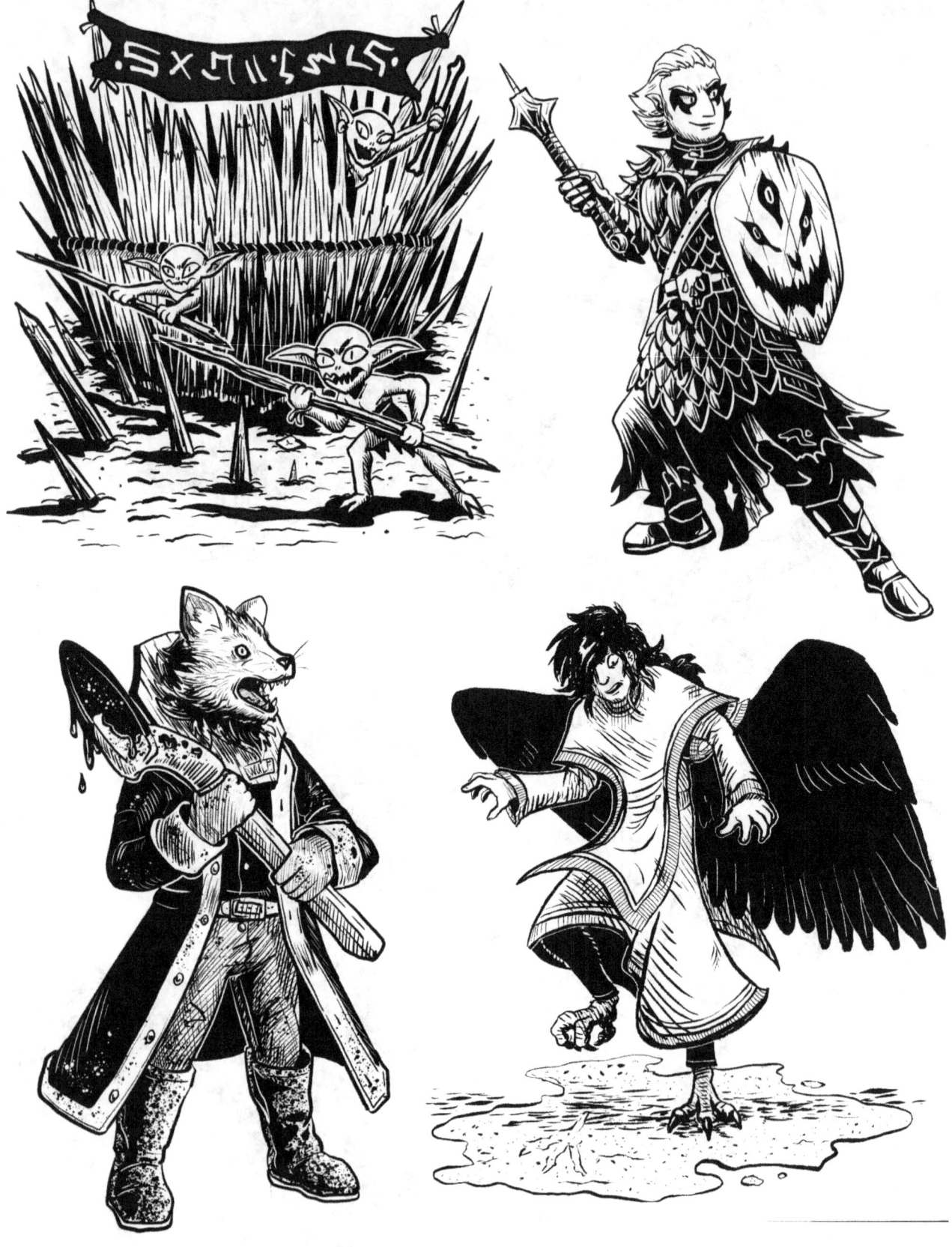

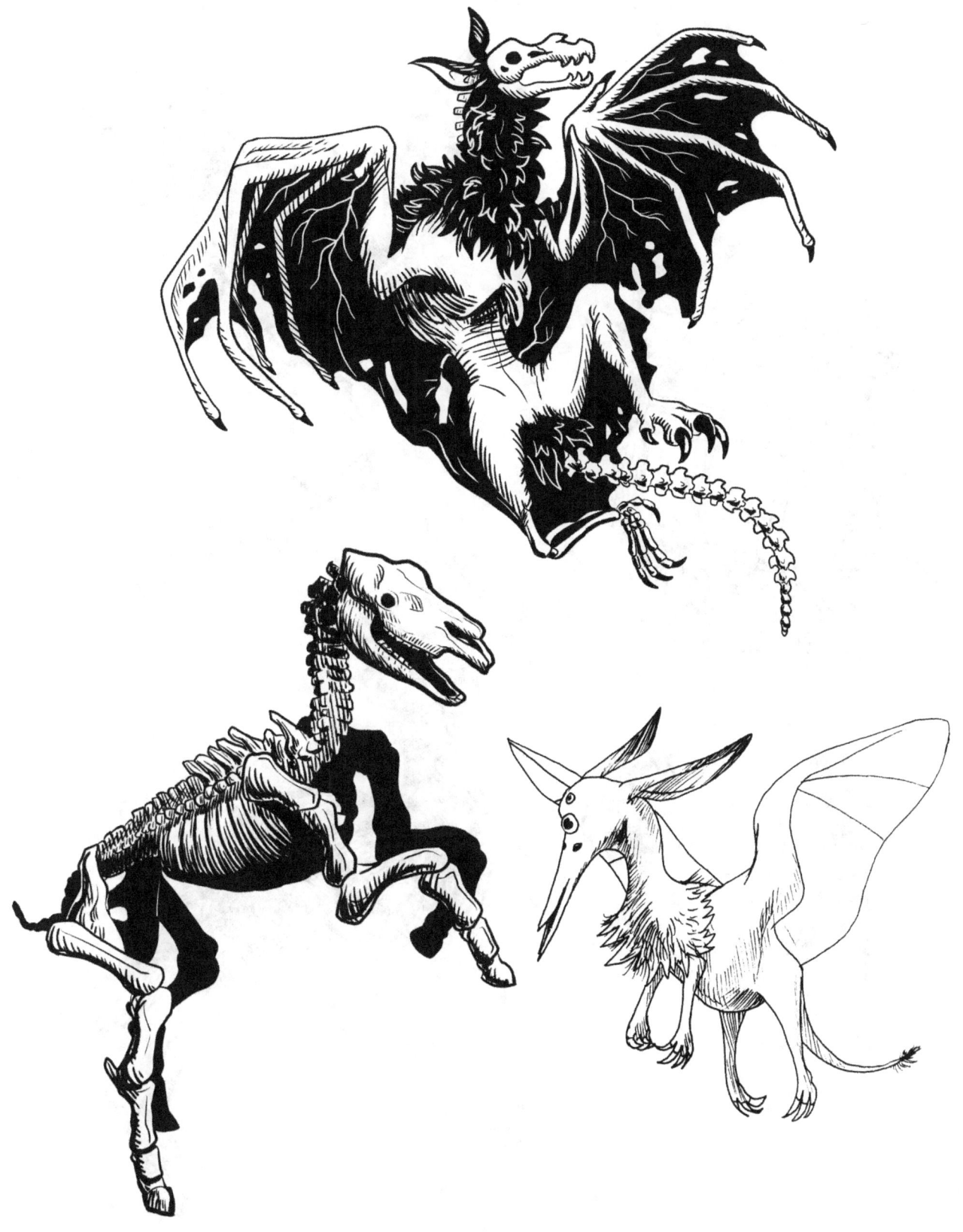

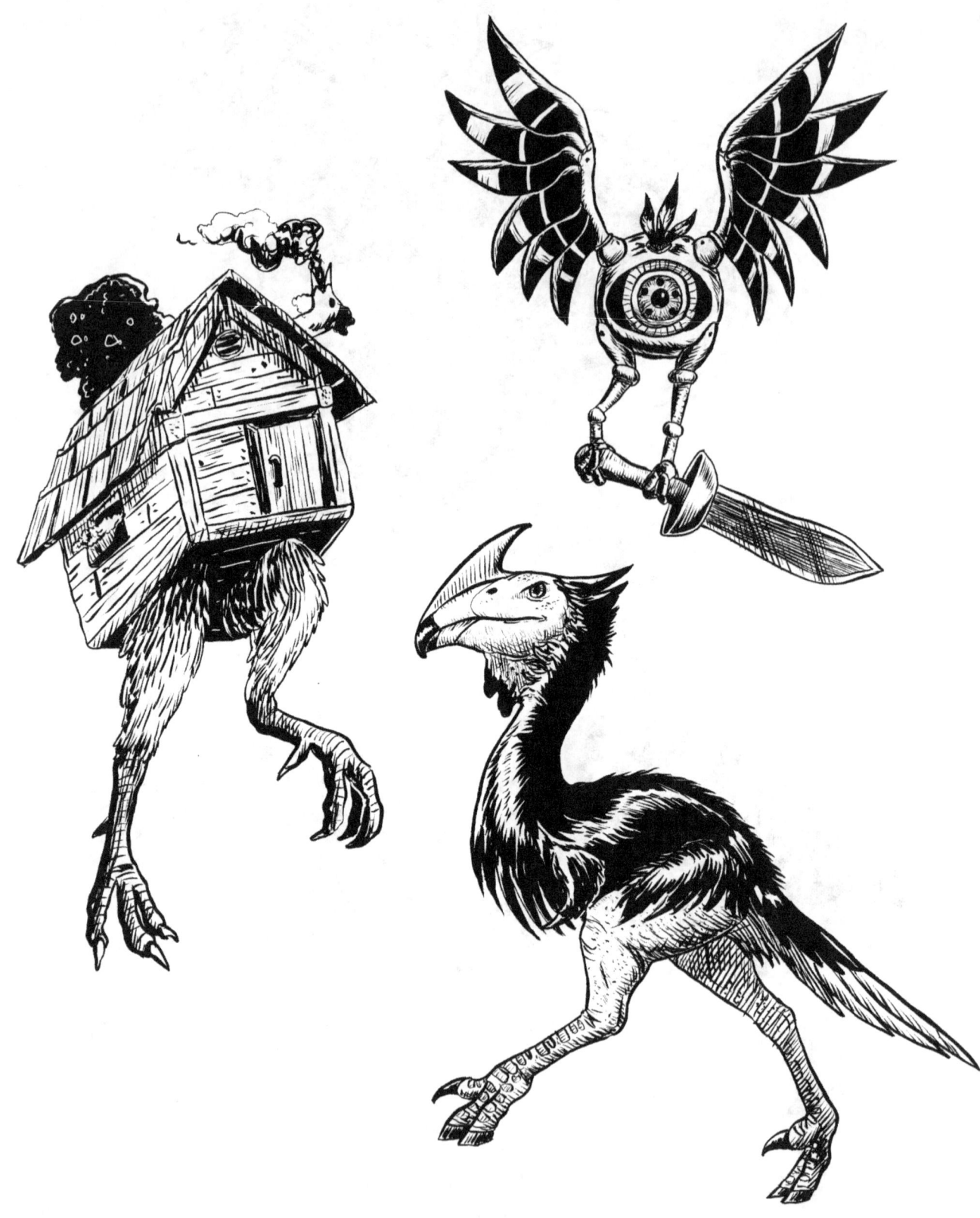

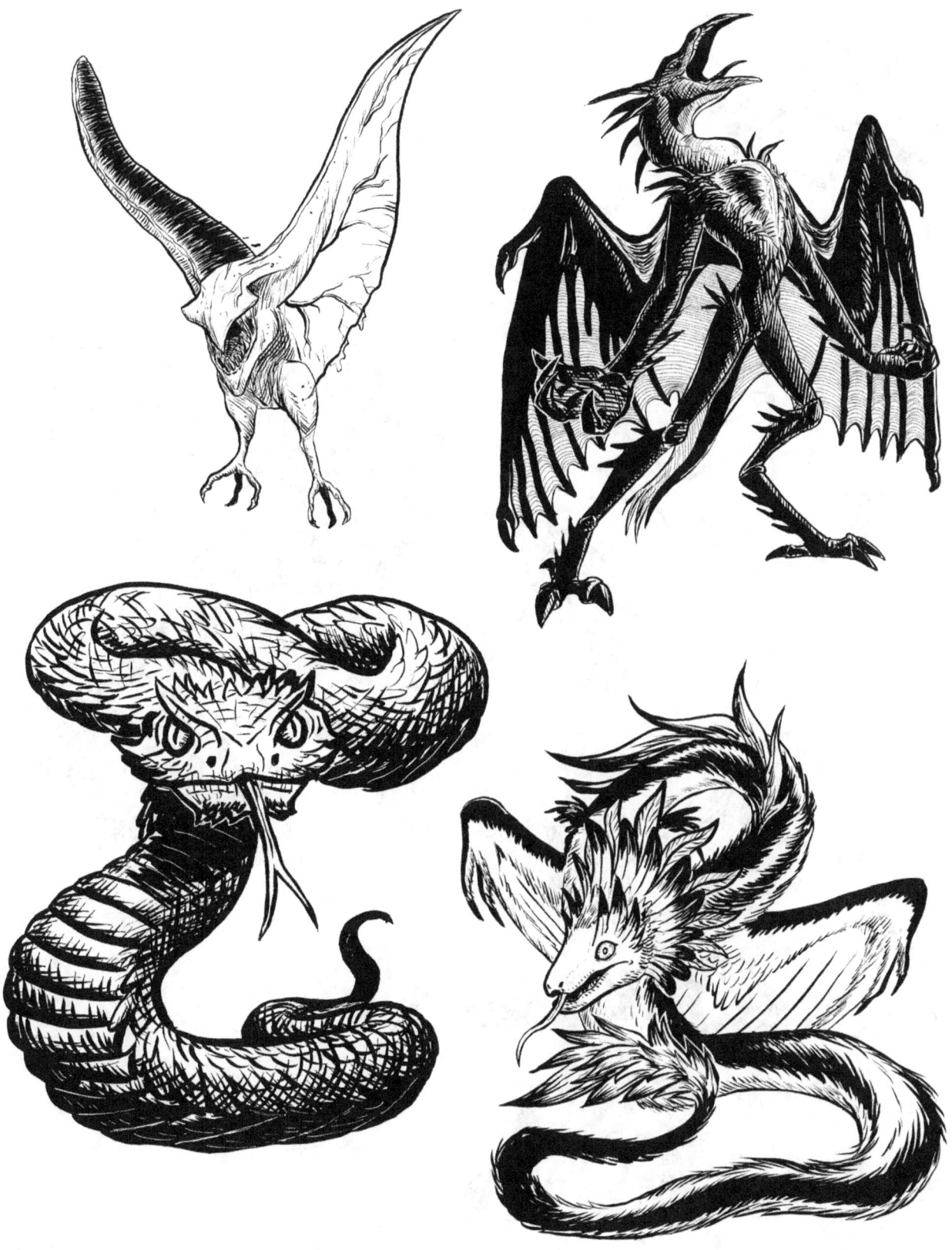

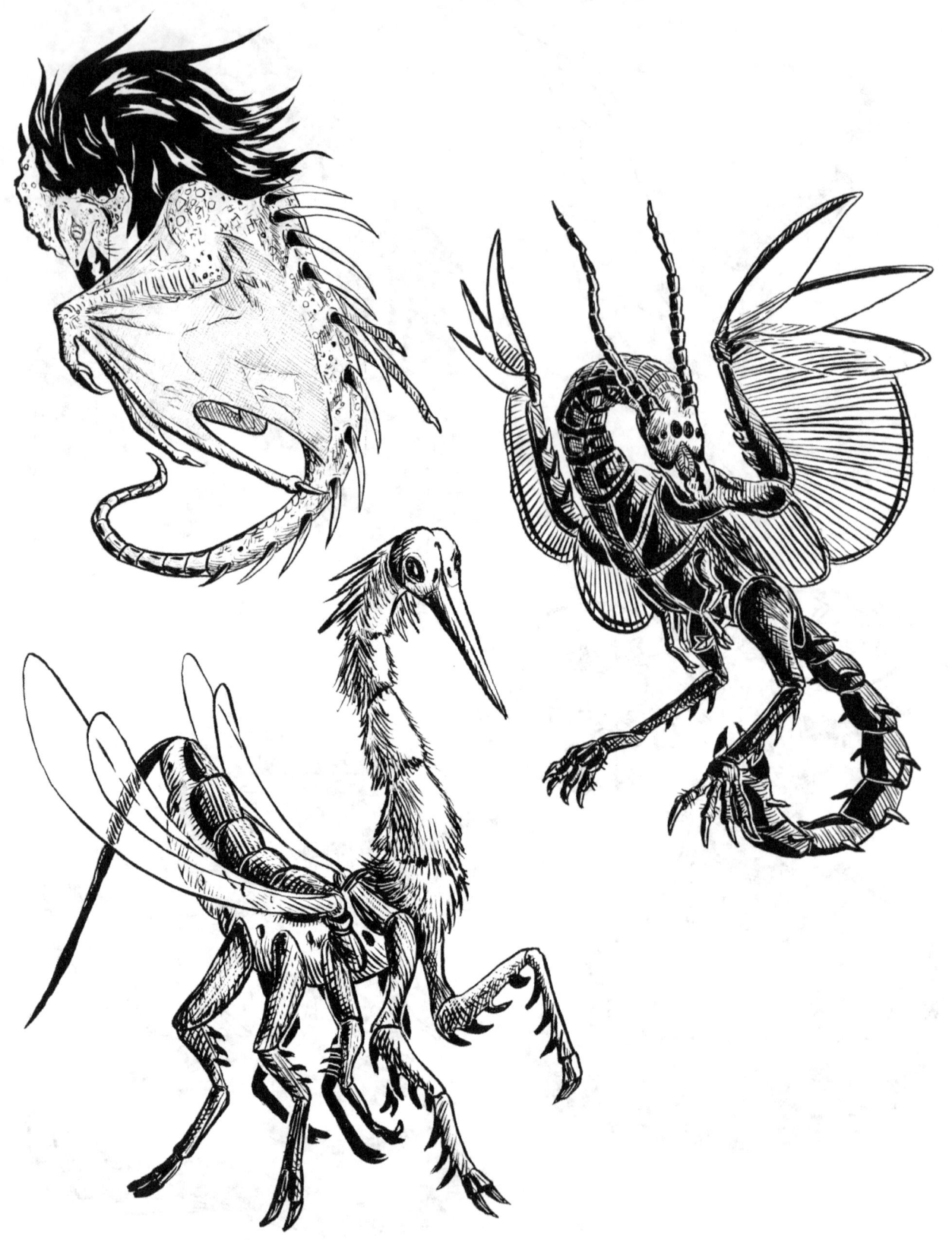

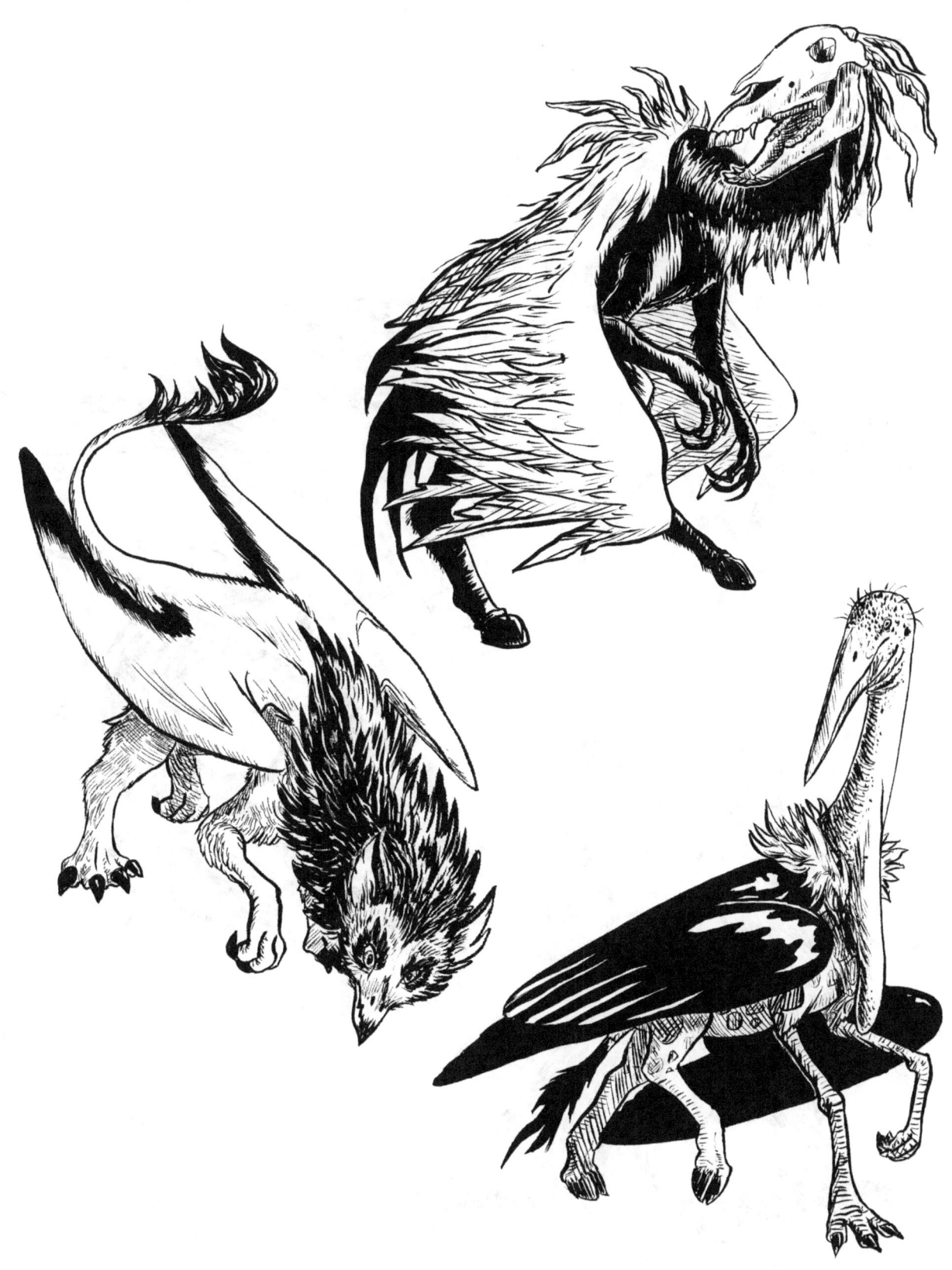

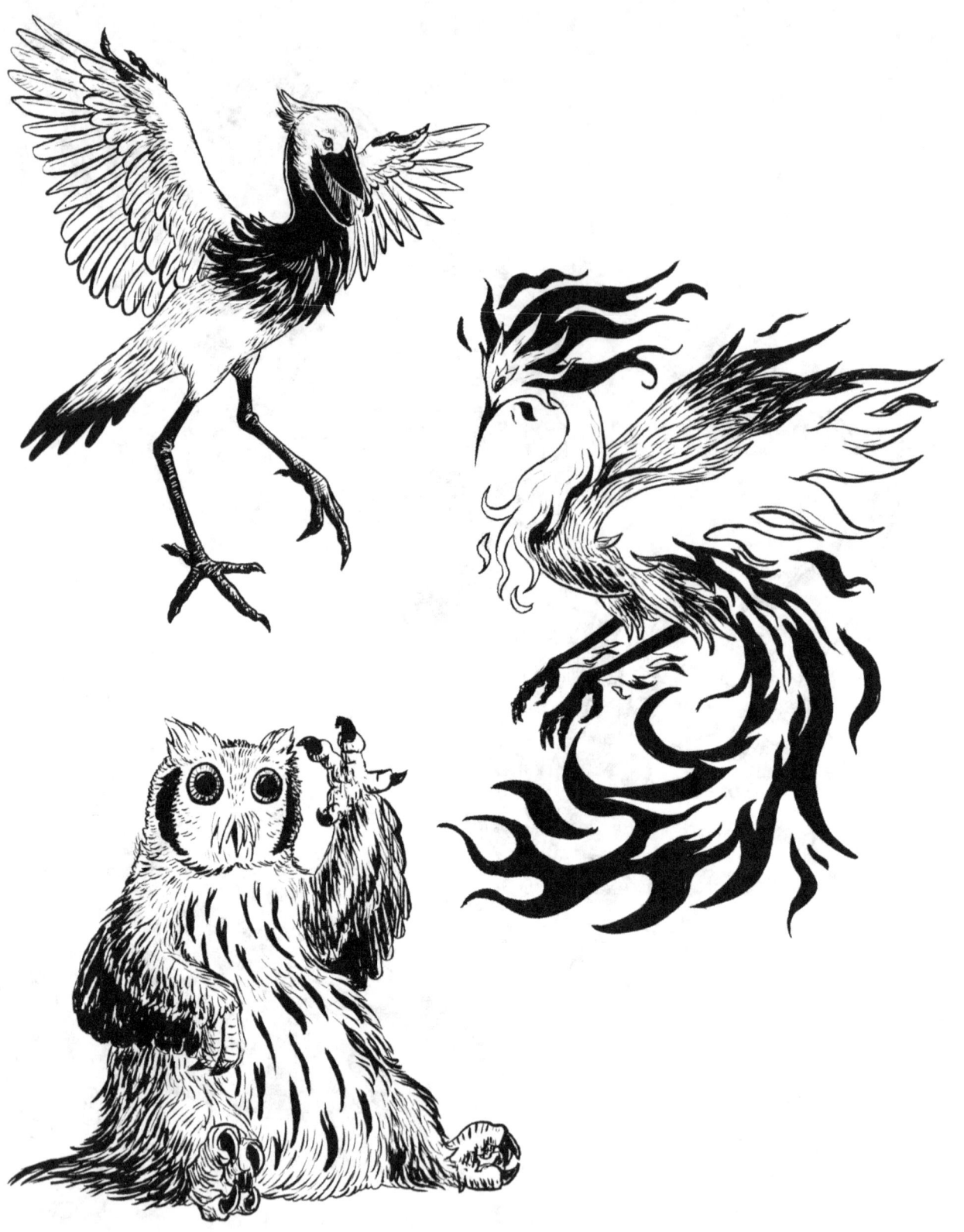

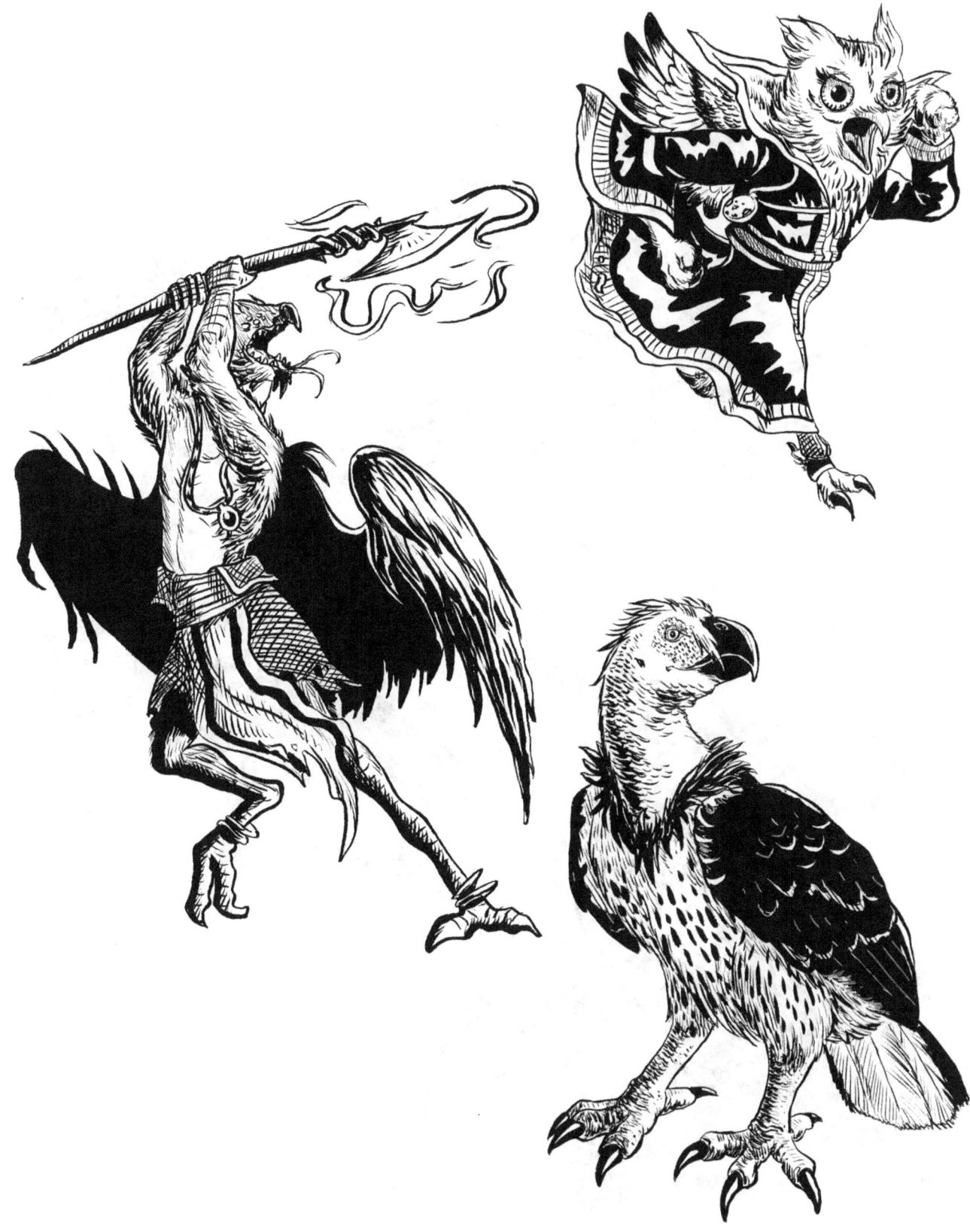

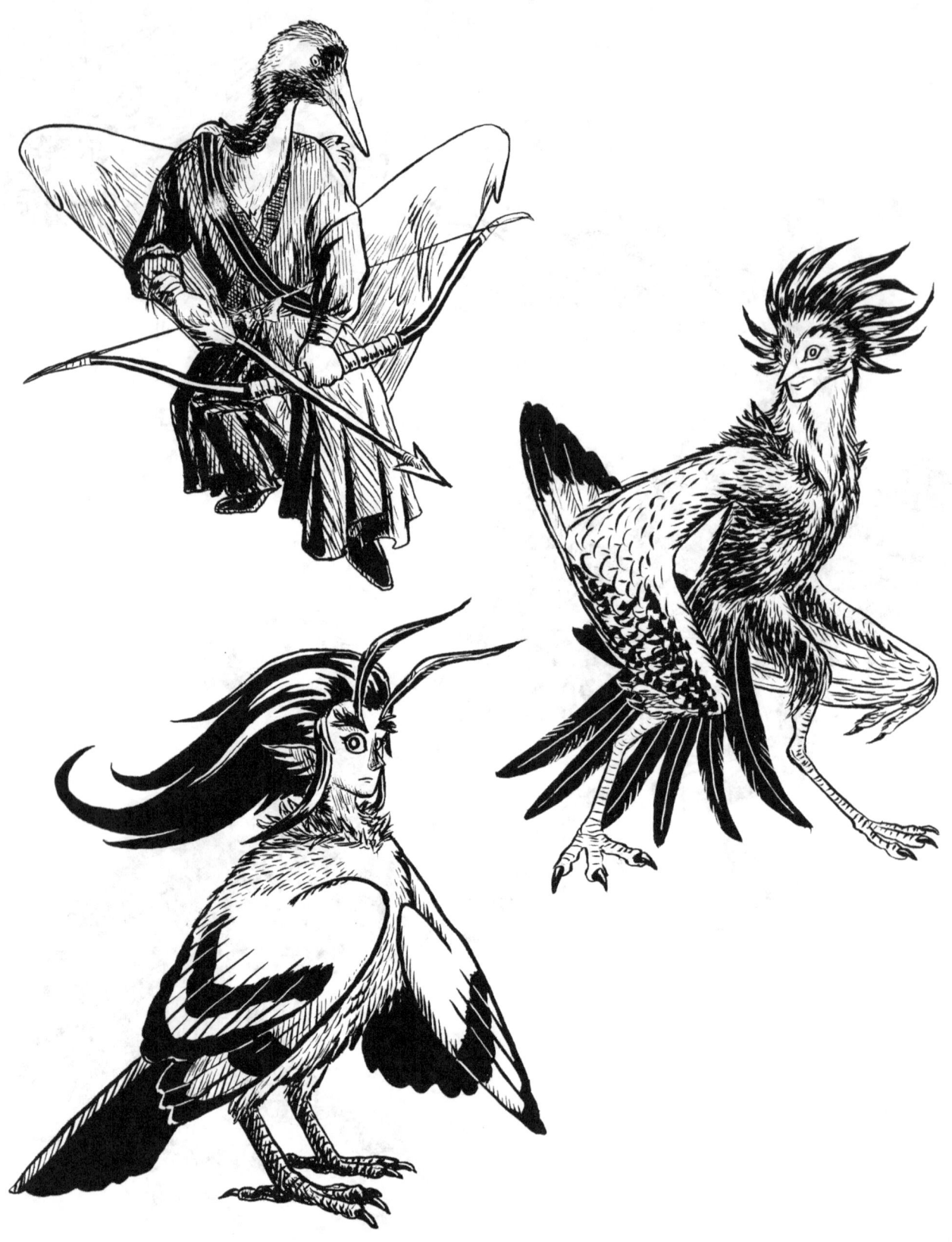

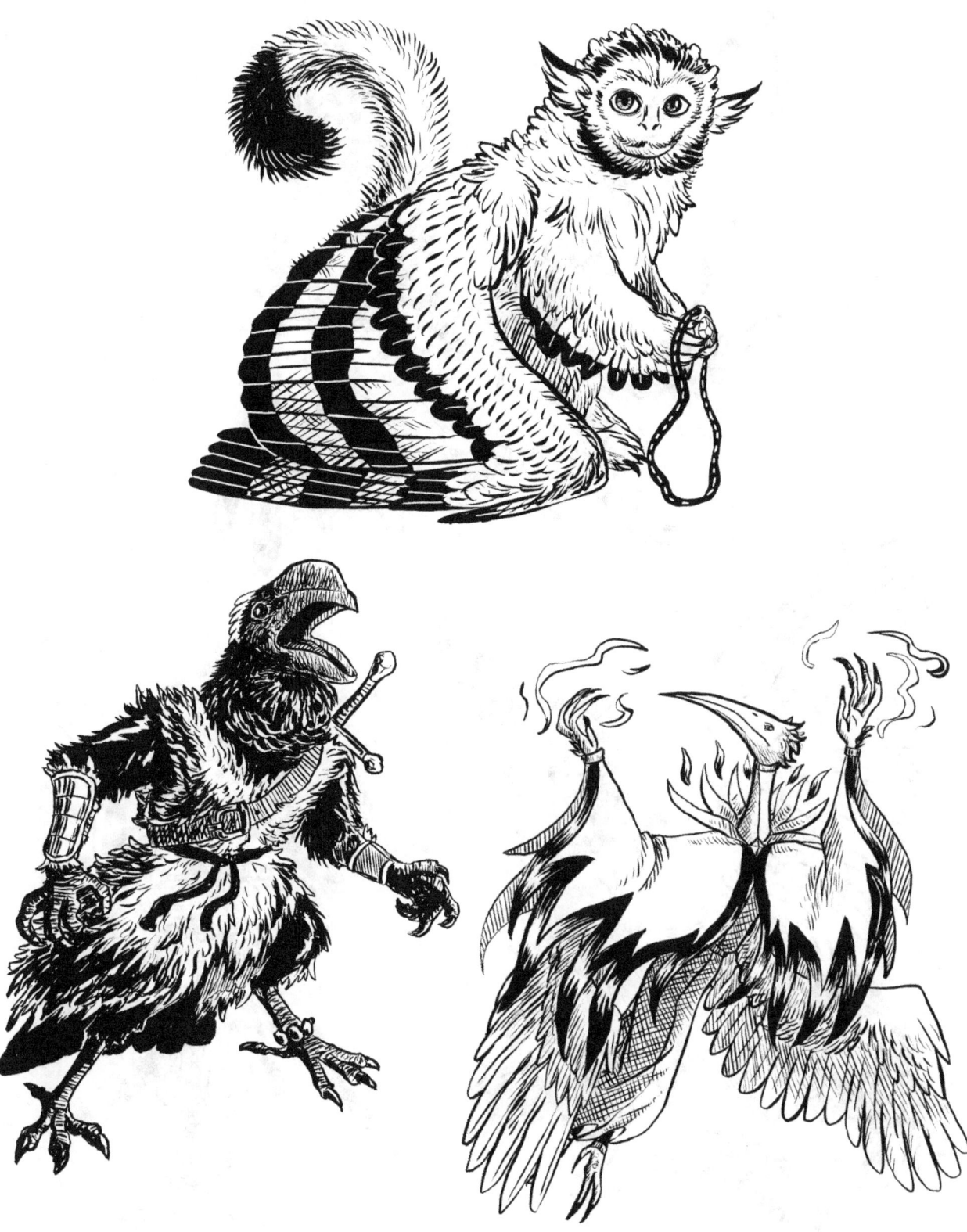

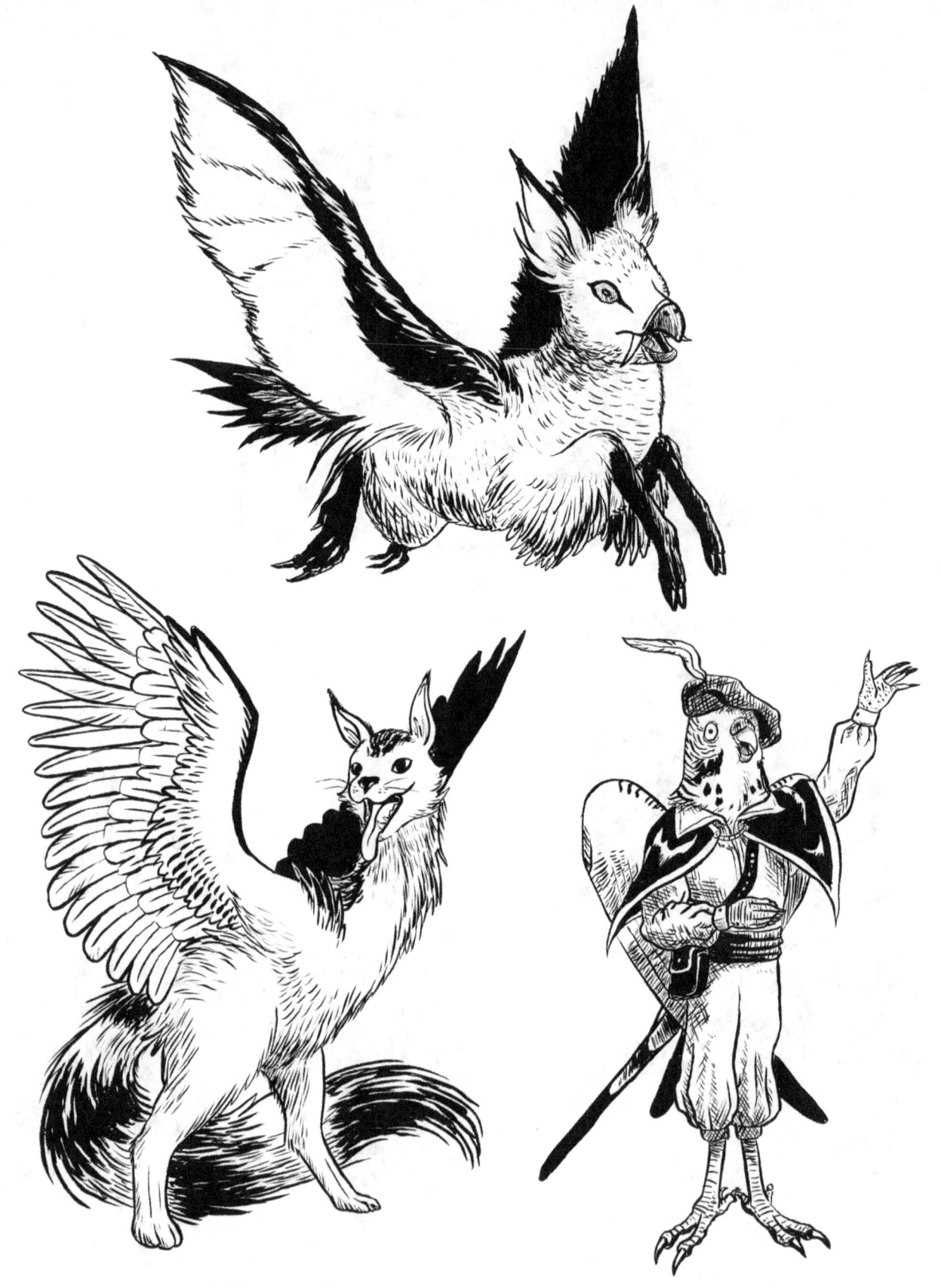

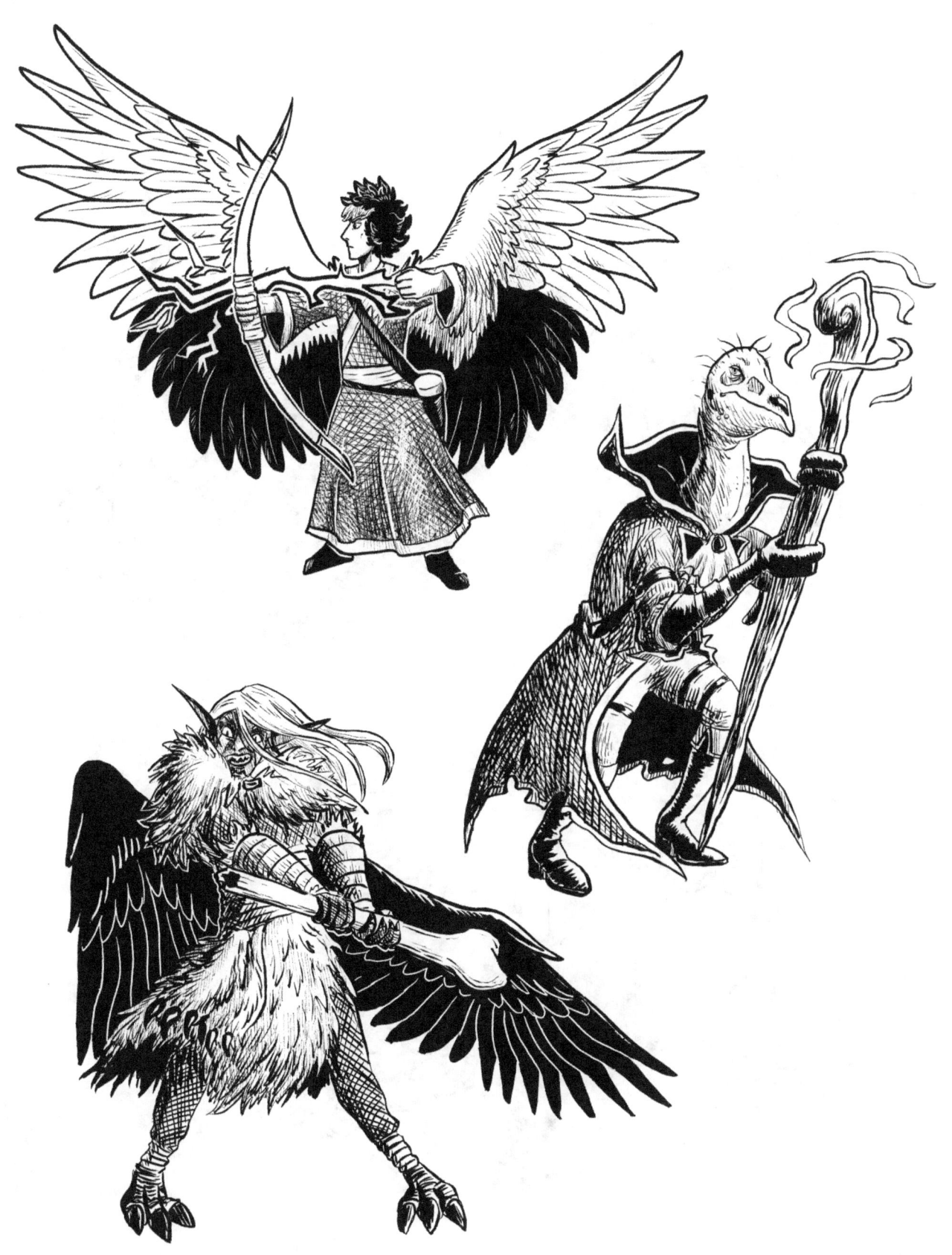

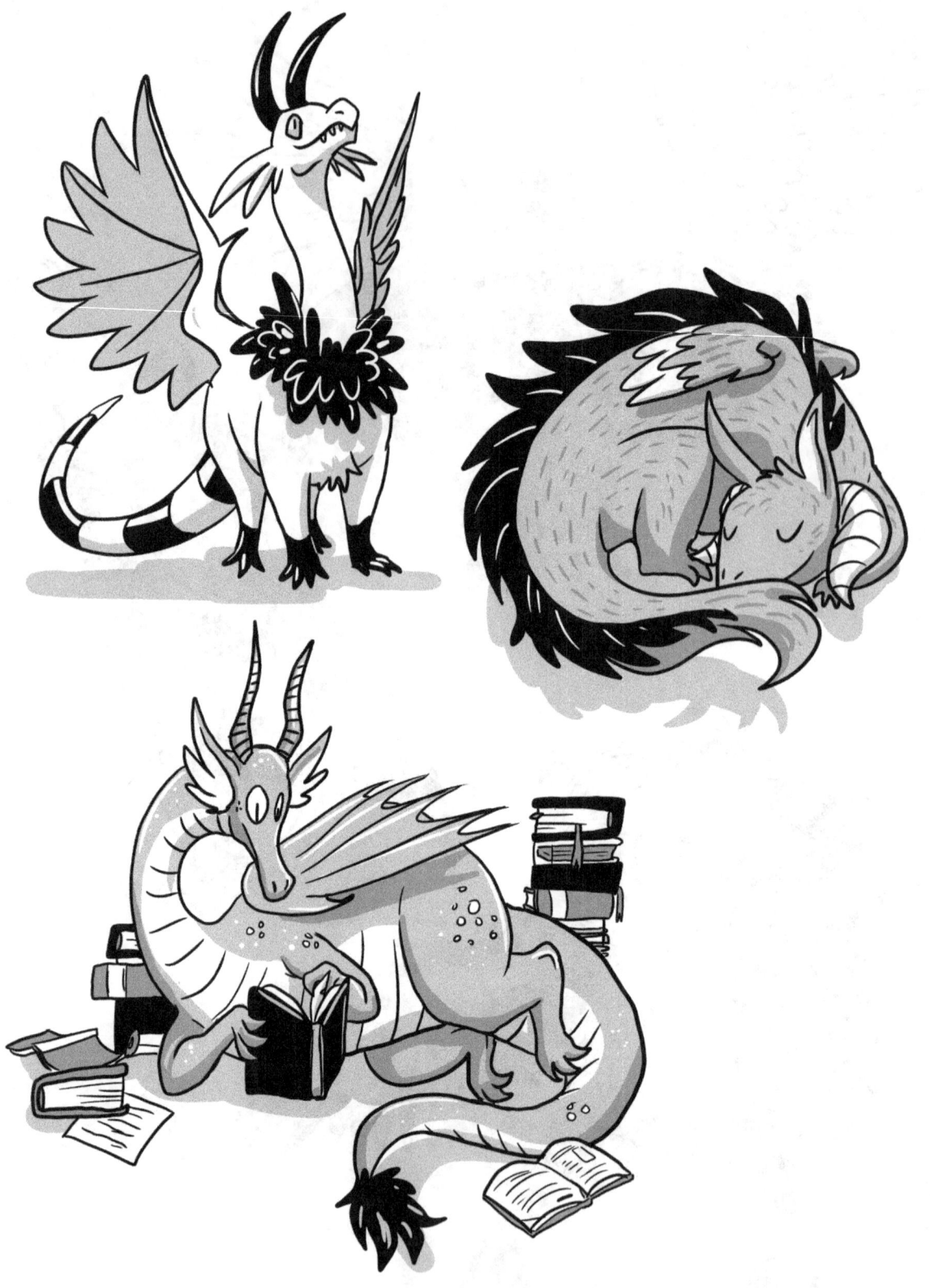

www.ingramcontent.com/pod-product-compliance
Lightning Source LLC
Chambersburg PA
CBHW082254220526
45469CB00009B/3000